SEXUAL IDENTITY

A Guide to Living in the Time Between the Times

Mark A. Yarhouse
Lori A. Burkett

University Press of America,® Inc.
Lanham · Boulder · New York · Toronto · Oxford

4501 Forbes Boulevard
Suite 200
Lanham, Maryland 20706
UPA Acquisitions Department (301) 459-3366

PO Box 317
Oxford
OX2 9RU, UK

Printed in the United States of America
British Library Cataloging in Publication Information Available

ISBN 0-7618-2603-3 (paperback : alk. ppr.)

™ The paper used in this publication meets the minimum
requirements of American National Standard for Information
Sciences—Permanence of Paper for Printed Library Materials,
ANSI Z39.48—1984

To Lori Yarhouse, sacred companion on the journey,
and in memory of Cecelia ("Took") and Ken Thomas
—Mark

In loving memory of Lora Peyton Vaughan
and Anne Langley Beaman
—Lori

Contents

Acknowledgments

This book would not have been written had we not each spent several years working with people who struggled with homosexuality. Some of these courageous people specifically asked that their stories be told. For example, one man, after he was asked if we could include some of his experiences in this book, stated, "Please share my story. If there is anything about the struggles I have been through that would benefit others, I want to offer it."

There are many similar men and women whose stories we share throughout this book. Each name has been changed to protect their identity, but we want to acknowledge our indebtedness to their courage and hard work.

The focus in this book on sexual identity arose out of a paper Mark first presented at the *Christian Scholarship...for What? International, Interdisciplinary Conference* at Calvin College in Grand Rapids, Michigan, in September of 2001. We would like to thank Susan Felch for inviting Mark to coordinate a session on sexual identity concerns, and we thank David Myers for his response to Mark's paper and Wayne Joosse for chairing the session. The paper—titled "Sexual identity development: The influence of valuative frameworks on identity synthesis"—was re-worked and eventually published in *Psychotherapy*, a peer-reviewed journal now published by the American Psychological Association.

Chapters 1 through 3 introduce the reader to a number of issues. Much of the thinking that informs the theological perspectives and research-informed perspectives are indebted to past work with Stanton L. Jones, and these issues are developed even further in *Homosexuality: The Use of Scientific Research in the Church's Moral Debate* (published by InterVarsity Press).

The central chapters are born out of our clinical experience working with men and women who enter professional therapy distressed by their same-sex attraction experiences. Most of the men and women we have worked with feel they contend with same-sex attraction—"contend" because they do not feel that the attractions reflect "who they are" as a person. Some of the material presented here was originally developed for the therapist workbook, *Expanding Alternatives to Same-Sex Attraction and Behavior: Clinical Modules for Informed Consent, Assessment, and Intervention* (available from Mark A. Yarhouse).

The final section reflects our concern that the issues discussed in this book need to be addressed at the broader levels of family and church community. It is not enough to point people in the direction of helpful resources and to then allow their brothers and sisters to struggle in isolation. Ours is a call for a more intentional shift in focus to help those who contend with same-sex attraction and wish to live a chaste life.

We want to express our indebtedness to many of our colleagues at Regent University who have made that institution a rich place for Christian scholarship. In particular, we want to thank Bill Hathaway for making the Doctoral Program in Clinical Psychology a place that stimulates critical thinking in a variety of areas in psychology. We want to recognize the Initiative for Healthy Sexuality at Regent University, a research team comprised of several doctoral students from the Doctoral Program in Clinical Psychology. Several students have spent countless hours working with us on marriage, family, and sexuality-related topics and have helped us think through some of the complicated issues that we address throughout this book. We want to especially thank Erica Tan, Lisa Pawlowski, Stephen Russell, Heather Brooke, Mel Jenkins, Sally Falwell, and Mary Alice Quinlan for their work and encouragement. We also want to recognize the Faculty Senate at Regent University for grant support of this project and related research over the last few years.

We would also like to thank Stanton L. Jones, Warren Throckmorton, and several anonymous reviewers for their comments on earlier versions of the manuscript. Also, we would like to thank Evelyn Still and Janet Cooper, our editors, for working with us on this project.

Mark also thanks his wife, Lori, and their children, Lynnea, Peter, and Celia, for all of their love and support. The encouragement they give him and the fellowship they share together is priceless. Peter, who is three, often worded his evening prayers these past few months as follows: "Thank you for Jesus. Thank you for Daddy. Help him at work. Have a good time. Amen."

Albert Camus once wrote, "In the depth of winter I finally learned that within me there lay an invincible summer." Lori wishes to thank her family and closest friends for their incredible support, faithfulness, and love during the depths of winter. You made discovering an invincible summer more meaningful and enjoyable. Lori would also like to thank Mark for his mentoring and leadership throughout this project.

Part 1:

Foundational Considerations

Chapter

1

Sexual Identity

Introduction

Perhaps you are wondering about the title of this book. What does it mean to *live* in the time between the times? A theologian once noted that the time period between Pentecost and the return of Christ is similar to the time period between D-day and V-day. During World War II, D-Day marked a significant turning point in the war against Germany. It became clear that the Allies would win the war, though the war was still far from over. While V-day marked the end of World War II, D-Day marked the beginning of the end. The experience between D-day and V-day is much like the Christians' experience in history. We know that victory is secured because of Christ's sacrifice and resurrection, yet we live in the middle of a battle until Christ's victory takes its final form. Mary Stewart Van Leeuwen, in her writing, referred to this period as the "time between the times."

Perhaps no group of people finds itself as much a casualty of a war that has already been won than those Christians who contend with same-sex attraction. After all, they believe Christ secured them victory, and they enjoy the knowledge of salvation. Yet, they also continue to struggle with homosexual desires, and they do not believe that these attractions reflect God's best for them.

This book is a resource for Christians who find themselves distressed and, at times, overwhelmed by their struggles with same-sex attraction. It is a book, then, for those who contend with same-sex attraction and want to live faithfully before God in all areas of their lives, including their sexuality and sexual behavior.

This book ultimately intends to support people who continue to suffer with issues concerning their sexual identity. By sexual identity we are referring to a person's (1) sense of gender as male or female, (2) sexual preference, for example, toward the same- or opposite-sex, and (3) behaviors or intentions in light of their sexual attraction.[1] These three components make up a person's sexual identity. By writing a book to help people who struggle with their sexual identity, we are not primarily focusing on helping people change their sexual orientation, though sexual orientation or sexual preference is one of the three main things that make up sexual identity. So we do not ignore sexual orientation, but we are not focusing exclusively on changing it either.

In this book we attempt to take a broader view (sexual identity) rather than a more narrow view (sexual orientation). Perhaps you are aware that several conservative religious organizations recently pooled their resources to take out full-page advertisements in several major newspapers stating that homosexual persons can experience a complete change of sexual orientation. Why isn't this book a resource to help people do just that? There are many answers to this question; let us offer you two.

The first answer is that there are several books written by "ex-gay" persons and ministry leaders who share their experiences coming out of homosexuality.[2] They write about how they experienced a change of sexual orientation, and they offer suggestions for how readers might proceed. While these are valuable resources for those who pursue a change of orientation, what is missing from the resources on this topic is a book for those who either are in the process of change, yet continue to experience same-sex attraction, or for those who have been through such a program of change and continue to experience same-sex attraction despite their best efforts.

Consequently several resources written by people who say they have experienced a change of sexual orientation are already available. However, there is a second reason for writing this book. Research published on change of sexual orientation suggests that many people who pursue change of orientation will achieve only partial success. That is, most people will experience less success than they may have desired. By "orientation" most people mean the *directionality* of a person's attractions toward the opposite sex, the same sex, or both. Most people who attempt to change this directionality will be less successful than they desired. Despite all of their efforts, most people who pursue change will still have same-sex attraction experiences.

This is a sobering statement for conservative religious communities to face. If we go to the studies published to date, however, we find the success rate for attempting change is at approximately 30 percent, with a few studies lower and a few studies higher.[3] This is considered relatively low when compared to treatment for depression, for example, which has a success rate of closer to 70 percent. When compared to marital therapy or treatment of substance abuse, it is not too far off the mark. What this suggests is that just as most people who contend with substance abuse may continue to struggle throughout their lives, so too most people who experience same-sex attraction may contend with these proclivities for a lifetime.

Let us qualify what we are saying. We know there are identified therapy approaches and techniques used to promote change in orientation. Unfortunately, we really do not know the actual success rate for participating in therapy to change one's sexual orientation. The studies conducted thus far to help us understand this success rate utilized poor methodologies. Better methods of measuring change might lead to a higher success rate; but better methods may also lead to a lower success rate. What appears to be true at this time is that while some people report success in experiencing change of orientation, many people report only partial success. The majority of people who attempt a change of behavior report being able to change their behavior, yet still struggle with experiences of same-sex attraction. That is, most people who attempt to live a chaste life and not act on their same-sex attractions report success in doing so.[4] This makes intuitive sense. Orientation is much more complicated than behavior.

Sexual Orientation

Sexual orientation refers to the *direction* of a person's attractions. Scientists and researchers propose a number of theories about what causes a person to experience same-sex attraction or to have a homosexual orientation. The bottom line is that scientists do not really know for certain why one person experiences same-sex attraction and another does not. The competing theories tend to fall into one of two camps. Do you remember the old "Nature vs. Nurture" debate you probably discussed in school? Well, some propose that same-sex attraction is due primarily to Nature, that biology—through genetics or exposure to prenatal hormones—contributes to same-sex attraction. Others claim it is Nurture. People on the Nurture side of the debate tend to believe that parent-child relationships contribute to experiences of same-sex attraction, or that being sexually abused as a child can contribute to same-sex desire later in life. These are theories, not facts. Let us consider some of the evidence for each, while making it clear that we really do not know for sure.

Earlier studies of twins reported that identical twins were more likely than fraternal twins to both be homosexual as adults. However, more recent research has suggested that evidence for this theory is not nearly as strong as was originally thought. Similarly, research on a chromosomal marker initially suggested a genetic marker for homosexuality, yet follow-up research has not confirmed this, and in one case the researchers could not find the marker at all. Similar problems appear when we consider the evidence for Nurture or the environment shaping our sexual identity. Research on parent-child relationships has been mixed and somewhat confusing. Some studies appear to support the theory, while others do not. Most experts today believe that both Nature and Nurture contribute to a person's experience of same-sex attraction. The specifics vary from person to person.

Sexual Identity

We mentioned earlier that sexual identity refers to a person's sense of their gender (as male or female), their sexual orientation or preference, and what they choose to do with the attractions they have. So when we consider one of these three aspects of sexual identity, sexual orientation, we are suggesting that people have little say over whether they experience same-sex attractions to begin with. If you are experiencing same-sex attractions or believe you have a homosexual orientation, we believe it is not something you did or failed to do that led you to have these attractions. However, it is clear that a person can choose to act on or refrain from acting on their attractions. This is a second dimension to sexual identity: What you do with the attractions you have—an important component to our approach to sexual identity. The third dimension to sexual identity is your sense of being either male or female. In our approach, you also can explore your sense of being male or female and the extent to which you identify with your gender.

Sexual identity is influenced by your self-appraisal, sexual interests, thoughts, fantasies you cultivate, and your intentions for sexual behavior. We are not suggesting you give up on changing your sexual orientation, but we want to expand your focus so you are not overly consumed with your sexual orientation at the expense of the many other dimensions of your sexual identity and sense of yourself as a person.

In our counseling experience, we have found that many Christians have become discouraged after attempting to change their sexual orientation. They believe they should be able to change their sexual orientation, then end up having only partial success, which they interpret either as failure, not having enough faith, or not having tried hard enough.

When this happens, people find themselves at the proverbial fork in the road. We might say that when a person's expectations for change are not met, they are left with a choice. Most people are faced with the following choices: They can (a) reinvest time and energy in working a program designed to change their sexual orientation, (b) discontinue their focused attempts to change their orientation and maintain a chaste lifestyle, or (c) discontinue their attempts to change their sexual orientation and pursue a same-sex relationship.

This book provides another option altogether. It lies somewhere between options (a) and (b), above. We invite people who experience same-sex attraction to focus less on changing their sexual orientation (rather than reinvest or discontinue altogether) and more on living faithfully before God while still experiencing same-sex attraction. This is a focus more on sexual identity, which includes, but is not limited to, your sexual orientation.

Designed as a practical resource, this book is for those people who do not experience a complete change of sexual orientation despite their best efforts. This is perhaps the single most unique aspect of this book. Its goal is not to focus on exclusively helping people change their sexual orientation. But what are the goals of this book, if not to change a person's sexual orientation? The goals of this book are to provide support and practical assistance to devout Christians who have attempted to change their sexual orientation but, thus far, have had partial success. At the most concrete and practical level, our goals are to have you:

1. Increase your understanding of the many influences on your current experiences of same-sex attraction and behavior,
2. Recognize the relationships among physical sensations, thoughts, feelings, and behavior,
3. Improve how you plan your daily routine and schedule to help you manage experiences of same-sex attraction,
4. Reduce the frequency and intensity of same-sex attraction and behavior,
5. Have a firm sense of your identity that is consistent with your life goals,
6. Identify spiritual resources that facilitate your life goals, particularly as you live out a practical theology of sanctification, and
7. Explore your capacity for relating to others in emotionally meaningful ways, while you maintain the freedom to achieve chastity in relationships.

Beyond these goals we also hope this book will offer concrete and practical suggestions for how family members and the church might truly relate as the Body of Christ to those who contend with same-sex attraction.

When we refer to the intended audience of *devout Christians*, we are pointing to those Christians who are orthodox in their affirmation of the Christian sexual ethic. The Christian sexual ethic is that God's revealed will for human sexuality is that full sexual intimacy occurs in marriage between a husband and wife. Although this may be seen with reference to creation, this sexual ethic is affirmed throughout Scripture and over two millennia of Christian instruction. So devout Christians struggle with their experiences of same-sex attraction precisely because they do not see these experiences as in keeping with God's revealed will for human sexuality. They do not want to change their beliefs about who God is and what God says about sexual ethics. If they cannot experience a change of sexual orientation, they desire to arrange their lives in such a manner that they can live faithfully to their understanding of God's call on their lives as persons created in the image of God.

What do we mean when we refer to devout Christians *who have attempted to change their sexual orientation but have been unable to thus far?* In our experience, most people who experience homosexual attractions have attempted to change these attractions at some point in their lives. Many pray that God remove these same-sex attractions. They may identify with Paul when he petitioned God three times to remove his "thorn in the flesh" (2 Cor. 12:7-9). A number of believers participate in more extensive ministry or therapy hoping to experience a change of their sexual orientation. It is our belief that most people who experience same-sex attraction—even those who may now identify as gay, lesbian, or bisexual—have at one time attempted to change their orientation, many of them looking to God to bring about that change.

Is This the Best Fit for Me?

It is important to note that this book may not be the best fit for everyone. First, you may be in the rigorous process of attempting to change your sexual orientation and desire to continue on that path. The vast majority of persons who report a change of orientation also report that that change took time. In one study, the average length of time for attempting a change before the onset of any change was *two years*, with conviction that change occurred at upwards of *five years*.[5] So the change process, when successful, appears to take a period of time. We cannot designate what constitutes *enough time* invested in reorientation therapy. Perhaps you are invested in that process but did not realize its length, yet you want to continue to work a specific program. We want to encourage you in your efforts to change, as well as encourage you to be open to better methods to bring about that change. Although the focus of this book is not on changing sexual orientation, it may be useful as an additional resource as you attempt a rigorous program of change.

Also, this book may not be a good fit for you if you have changed your views on the Christian sexual ethic. Those of you who may have been involved in a change program for some time and are discouraged by the lack of progress, may already have made the decision that you can live faithfully before God while pursuing a same-sex relationship. We urge you to reflect on this decision. We cannot determine for you whether you have given it your *best effort*, but we do believe that a broader focus is needed. And we invite you to consider another perspective on sexual identity. We know from cognitive psychology research that when people feel "cognitive dissonance" between what they *believe* and what they *do*, they are much more likely to change what they believe. Living by one's principles is much more difficult than changing one's principles.

In any case, there are resources available to support those who change their view on the Christian sexual ethic, but this book attempts to focus more broadly on your sexual identity and the issues faced by those with only partial success in their attempts to change their sexual orientation.

For those who believe this resource may offer support and instruction, we turn now to a model of sexual identity development. This may provide a different way of thinking about your life trajectory, the path you are taking yourself down, or the path you feel God is taking you down.

Sexual Identity Development

As you contemplate where you are in your own journey, it may be important to consider particular models of sexual identity development. We recently proposed a model of sexual identity development and synthesis you may find helpful.[6] The model has five stages: (1) identity confusion/crisis, (2) identity attribution, (3) identity foreclosure, versus identity expansion, (4) identity reappraisal, and (5) identity synthesis. As you read through a brief description of each stage, you may want to consider where you find yourself amidst these stages.

The initial stage, *identity confusion or crisis*, is consistent with many other models of gay or lesbian identity development, and it is characterized by the confusion of experiencing attraction to members of the same sex in a predominantly heterosexual society. Some people experience this as a kind of crisis; others do not.

For example, a young teenager (we will identify as Scott), along with his parents, recently visited Mark. Scott acknowledged experiences of same-sex attraction, and his parents entreated Mark to "change" him. In therapy, many issues were raised. Scott, in light of his experiences of same-sex attraction, was uncertain about what kind of help he wanted. Part of him wanted to pursue a relationship; another part wanted the feelings to go away. Still another part did not want to deal with the thoughts and feelings at all, at least not until he was older. Because he was experiencing a great deal of confusion, Scott had not yet made self-defining attributions such as, "I am gay," although his parents were beginning to make such attributions and were worried that he needed treatment to change his orientation. Certainly, Scott was experiencing sexual identity confusion in light of his experiences of same-sex attraction, and this confusion was magnified in part by his parents' inability to acknowledge his struggle and present identity crisis.

Whether it happens immediately or over time, people make an *identity attribution* in light of having experiences of same-sex attraction. Some attribute their experiences of same-sex attraction to an emerging gay, lesbian, or bisexual identity; others do not see their proclivities as "who they are" as a person, but as one dimension of a personal identity. The contours of this alternative identity may be shaped by personal values, cultural beliefs, religious beliefs, messages from the media or entertainment industries, or some other influence on whether same-sex attractions lead to a self-defining attribution. For example, the entertainment and media portrayal of adolescents often suggests to a teen that "if you feel gay, you *are* gay." Over time this can shape a person's sexual identity.

Scott, the young teenager introduced above, had not yet defined himself publicly or privately as either gay or straight. He simply was confused and needed some assurances of acceptance from his parents before working toward any particular goal with respect to his sexual identity and behavior.

The third stage of sexual identity development is that of *identity foreclosure versus identity expansion.* Some individuals adopt a gay identity and then begin to synthesize that identity by either experimenting with same-sex relationships or being involved in peer groups that support same-sex identity and behavior. Others seek to expand their identity and look for alternatives to same-sex attraction and behavior. Some do so with a premature commitment that diminishes over time, while others reflect a kind of sustained resolve to an alternative life trajectory away from gay, lesbian, and bisexual identification.

This is an important point that must not be overlooked. Sometimes people are overly eager in their attempts to dis-identify with their experiences of same-sex attraction. They choose to cut themselves off from their attractions, without fully realizing they have essentially severed a dimension of their sexual experience. We will discuss this in greater detail later, but what is germane to the present discussion is that those who attempt this kind of amputation may not be fully prepared for a life of chastity, and may pursue a change of orientation only to find such change impossible for them by natural means. Such discouragement may lead them to conclude that the promises of the church and of various ministries are simply lies.

A life of chastity is a major life decision, and many devoted Christians rush into such a decision without first counting the costs of such a decision. Those individuals who do weigh this carefully and choose a life of chastity, resolve to live their life based on their understanding of the Christian sexual ethic. They then realize that though they struggle at times, they will not be abandoned in their efforts to live as they believe God would have them live.

Based upon a person's experience of satisfaction or success with either identity foreclosure or identity expansion, he or she may go through a time of *identity reappraisal* and, if their experiences have not been fulfilling, may even revert to a stage of confusion or crisis. While some people leave the gay lifestyle and enter a period of identity confusion, others discontinue their identity expansion, finding they prefer to integrate their experiences into a gay, lesbian, or bisexual identity. There are numerous reasons why people choose either direction. Ultimately, those who are satisfied with their sexual identity during the identity reappraisal stage decide on (generally speaking) one of two broad directions of identity synthesis. Either they continue in a model of gay, lesbian, or bisexual identity development, which typically involves exploration and disclosure, or they follow a path of identity development in the context of their beliefs and values.

What we are referring to here is *identity synthesis*, the final stage of our model of sexual identity development. Whatever the origins of same-sex attraction,[7] each person attributes their experiences of same-sex attraction to some larger meaningful script, eventually choosing how to live in light of their attributions. Some individuals report limited or moderate success with dis-identifying with their experiences of same-sex attraction and do not shape their identity around a core center of same-sex proclivity. Rather, they shape their identity around other aspects of who they are as a person.

It was mentioned earlier that this book is meant for those persons who are looking to explore and expand their sexual identity in light of ongoing experiences of same-sex attractions or partial success in their attempts to change their sexual orientation. In other words, the attractions have not gone away completely. At the same time, this book is for those who choose not to identify with those attractions, or who have decided that these attractions do not define who they are as a person. We now turn to the factors that may contribute to a person's *resolve* to dis-identify with their attractions and live their life in keeping with the Christian sexual ethic.

Factors which May Contribute to Resolve

Resolve is hard to come by. Our culture does not support it, and when the broader culture does not support an attribute or character trait, it makes it especially challenging to achieve or maintain it. There was a time in our society's history when personal resolve seemed valued as a quality or character trait. Determination mattered; it was part of what it meant perhaps to attain the so-called American Dream. Today, however, resolve and determination have lost ground to cynicism on the one hand and self-gratification on the other.

Fran White was one of the key figures at Wheaton College when the doctoral program in clinical psychology first began. She was a psychologist with an extensive background in missions; she was beloved by students and other faculty members alike. Fran once told Mark that cynicism is death to Christian vitality. It is amazing how a simple comment like this can have such an impact on a student. Fran was absolutely right. To be cynical is to essentially mock or sneer at the virtues or good intentions of others. In a culture that has all but lost heroes to admire and imitate, cynicism keeps us from appreciating the decision people make to live their lives according to a Christian sexual ethic. People are simply cynical toward those who refrain from a variety of sexual behaviors, including heavy petting, premarital sex, and same-sex behavior.

One thing that fuels cynicism is our culture's vision of self-gratification. Carl Rogers was once referred to as the "quiet revolutionary," because he brought a way of thinking about ourselves into our culture's consciousness. Rogers emphasized self-actualization as something to strive for and said that we will work toward such actualization if we are provided the right kind of environment, one that is unconditionally loving and empathic. He was a quiet revolutionary because few people today can trace their own valuing of self-gratification to any one source. They just find themselves valuing it or at least living as though it were a value. This happens in the church culture, too, where some Christians do not even realize they contend with self-gratification in its various forms as a way of orienting themselves to the world. They might question it only when brought to their attention.

In discussions of our sexuality, it is assumed that a person ought to pursue their own sexual self-gratification. Sexual expression has become a right rather than a gift from God. Sexual behavior becomes something I claim for myself (sexual self-gratification) rather than something that may have a claim on me.

Resolve or determination to live one's life by a sexual ethic, in this case the Christian sexual ethic, is then very difficult and flies in the face of many subtle (and many not-so-subtle) cultural pressures to do otherwise. In our experience, several factors may play a role in a person's ability to resolve to live a chaste life. These include the amount of same-sex attraction, experience in same-sex relationships, internal motivations, meaning making, and family and social support.

Amount of Same-Sex Attraction

One consideration that may impact a person's sense of resolve is the actual amount of same-sex attraction that person experiences. One way to look at this is to simply rate on a scale from 1–10 (with 1 meaning there is no same-sex attraction and 10 meaning there is strong same-sex attraction) your experience of same-sex attraction. You can do the same with your experiences of opposite-sex attraction (on a separate scale from 1–10 where 1 is no heterosexual attraction and 10 is strong heterosexual attraction).[8]

If a person sees that same-sex attractions predominate, they may struggle more with resolve than a person who has more opposite-sex attractions or even attractions. However, even a person who rates themselves as having strong same-sex attractions and no heterosexual attractions can work toward and maintain chastity, but they may struggle with more questions or doubts in the process.

For example, Mark recently corresponded with a woman who identifies herself as lesbian and who believes that her strong same-sex attractions suggest something to her about how she ought to live her life. She believes that these attractions function as a kind of moral compass pointing her in the direction of the kind of life she should lead, that is, she believes she should pursue a same-sex relationship. She also identifies herself as a Christian and believes in maintaining a monogamous relationship should she find the right partner. Although she claimed that the amount of same-sex attraction functions as a moral compass for how to live her life ("I'm just acting on the attractions that define me as a person."), this does not follow. It was C.S. Lewis, in *The Abolition of Man*, who noted that the fact that we have certain attractions says nothing about what we ought to do with them. We essentially have warring inclinations that require that we look outside of ourselves and beyond our inclinations or sexual attractions to a standard for conduct that informs us as to how we should live.

Experience in Same-Sex Relationships

A second potential factor is prior experience in same-sex relationships. One can imagine on the one hand a person who has same-sex thoughts and desires but has never acted on them. This person may be in a different place with respect to resolve when compared to someone who has been actively engaging in same-sex relationships over several years and with several partners. A person may also have been in one same-sex relationship over several years but later feels called to chastity. Fond memories may make resolve in that situation more challenging for that particular person.

As this suggests, resolve may take several forms. While the person with a more substantial sexual history may struggle more with going back to those experiences, he or she may also feel more resolved because of their experiences in specific relationships. Perhaps they had particularly negative experiences that make it easier for them to decide and commit to another path for themselves. Similarly, a person who has same-sex attractions but no experience may be drawn by their fantasies and struggle with resolve from that end; or they may be more resolved and have less of an inclination to participate in the gay community because they have not done so previously.

So prior experience in same-sex relationships is a consideration, but it is not a "one size fits all" factor. A person considering a sustained chaste life may benefit from reflecting upon their experiences (or lack thereof) and the impact of these on their life's trajectory.

Internal Motivations

Let us be clear at the outset that we do not believe that lack of motivation is the cause for most people not experiencing a change of sexual orientation. Many people try for years to change and are highly motivated to change to get married, save their marriage, maintain contact with their children, or for a variety of other reasons. This refers to the *amount* of motivation. But what we want to consider is the *kind* of motivation. When we think of motivations, we can distinguish between *external* and *internal* motivations. External motivations refer to those things we can point to as motivating us from outside of ourselves. For example, you might be motivated to work everyday so that you can pay off your mortgage or your car. These payments are what motivate you. These are external motivations for working. On the other hand, you could be motivated to work because you believe it is intrinsically rewarding. Perhaps you also believe your work is your calling, and that you are serving God when you serve others through your work. The fact that you can pay off your mortgage is a secondary benefit you receive from hard work, but it is not your primary motivation.

Our experience is that internal motivations are preferred to external motivations when it comes to responding to same-sex attraction. External motivations often take the form of an ultimatum from a spouse or pressure from one's parents or religious community. So a person enters therapy and states that if they did not come in for treatment, their wife would leave them; another person might state that her parents are making her come for help; still others enter therapy feeling pressure from their local church leadership. These pressures are real, but in our experience they are not the best motivation for chastity, since such a goal is lifelong and requires re-ordering your life in ways that can be quite demanding.

It seems to us much wiser to choose a life path based upon one's own beliefs and values. This way one's life path is internally rewarding. For the devout Christian, these are internalized motivations shaped and re-shaped by one's beliefs about God's intentions for human sexuality and sexual expression.

Meaning Making

People who contend with their experiences of same-sex attraction are essentially learning to cope with attractions that they have not chosen and that have not abated, despite their efforts at change. The idea of coping with stressful conditions is certainly not new, and there has been a growing body of literature on coping behaviors in response to both acute and chronic conditions of stress. A recently published model presents the relationship between meaning making and coping with a stressful condition.[9] We want to apply that model to the experience of persons who contend with same-sex attraction and show how the ability to make certain meanings may contribute to a person's ability to maintain resolve.

In our experience, people who seem to resolve themselves to living a chaste life make a connection between global meaning and situational meaning. *Global* meaning refers to a person's fundamental beliefs and basic assumptions about the world, including their sense of purpose and a sense for what is just and fair. *Situational* meaning refers to how a person's global beliefs interact around their own specific circumstances.

Let's consider the case of Sam (not his real name). When Sam began counseling, he identified himself as a Christian. He requested help dealing with his experiences of same-sex attraction, which he wanted to see himself rid of. He stated that if he could not experience change, he wanted to be equipped to live a chaste life consistent with the Christian sexual ethic. His global meaning as it pertained to his experiences of same-sex attraction influenced his understanding of his sexuality. He valued himself as a person and believed that the circumstances of this world were ultimately under the sovereign control of God. When he thought about his sexuality, he believed that his attractions were not his to act on, but that they were to be submitted to the will of God as God revealed His intentions regarding sexual expression.

This played itself out in the specific circumstances Sam was facing. When confronted with the experience of same-sex attraction at work or at church, for example, he made meaning out of his experiences of same-sex attraction with reference to the global meanings he had about human sexuality and sexual expression.

In terms of a person's ability to resolve themselves to live a chaste life, our experience is that appraisal of same-sex attraction and one's search for meaning is essential to a positive outcome. When people appraise or evaluate the meaning of their situation and find that it is personally meaningful or significant (insofar as it is the setting in which God has placed them and called them to obey), they place their attractions in relation to global meaning about God's revealed will for human sexuality. C.S. Lewis offers the following account of meaning making as it pertains to same-sex attractions:

> I take it for certain that the *physical* satisfaction of homosexual desires is sin. This leaves the [homosexual] no worse off than any normal person who is, for whatever reason, prevented from marrying.... our speculations on the cause of the abnormality are not what matters and we must be content with ignorance. The disciples were not told *why* (in terms of efficient cause) the man was born blind (Jn. IX 1-3): only the final cause, that the works of God [should] be made manifest in him. This suggests that in homosexuality, as in every other tribulation, those works can be

made manifest: i.e. that every disability conceals a vocation, if only we can find it...[10]

People who struggle in their meaning making experience incongruence between the situational meaning of experiencing same-sex attraction and the global meaning of what claim their sexuality has on their lives in light of God's sovereignty. Of course, the meaning we attach to certain situations, and certainly the global meanings we have, often develop in the context of our family and peer group, two other important considerations in one's experiences of resolve.

Family and Peer Group Support

Family and peer group support provide an important, practical dimension to a person's attempts to cope with same-sex attractions. Not only do we develop our sense of meaning in the context of these relationships, but we receive constant feedback in the form of support or criticism from those with whom we interact daily. If a family's or peer group's response is to reject a person who experiences same-sex attraction, even if they are attempting to live a chaste life, this rejection can be very difficult. The isolation that results may make it even more difficult to refrain from homosexual behavior. Also, it can be discouraging if a person is working toward chastity but interacting daily with friends and family who do not understand his or her desire to be chaste.

The opposite reaction from family and friends can be just as frustrating: Well-meaning family and friends may send the message that change is easy, that it involves a simple act of the will or a turning over of one's desires to God. These messages can create a tremendous amount of pressure in the person who has honestly been trying to change and who is now attempting to live a chaste life.

It is important to remember that these factors function as guidelines only, and they remind us that no two people are exactly alike in their struggle with any besetting condition. One person may be motivated by his spouse's ultimatum that he either get help or retain a lawyer, has little family or peer group support, and several years experience with same-sex partners. This is a much different experience from someone who may be motivated by deeply held religious beliefs and values about the moral status of same-sex behavior and has significant family and peer group support and no experience, apart from fantasies, in a same-sex relationship. Appropriate treatment goals may be to work toward chastity in his thought life. That is, to track patterns of same-sex attraction, the ways in which these patterns increase the likelihood of initial same-sex experimentation, and work on other developmental tasks of his stage of young adulthood, such as making meaningful connections with a small circle of peers who can encourage his religious faith and identity.

To summarize the foregoing, the most important consideration is that each person contending with same-sex attraction has his or her own story to tell. Each person has a different account of the ways in which these attractions are confusing, a concern, or in conflict with their beliefs or values. Some may be motivated by a family member's ultimatum; others may be deeply committed to chastity no matter what happens with regard to their sexual orientation.

Conclusion

This book places great emphasis on being concrete and practical. Although there is certainly a theological basis for this book—a basis absolutely foundational for understanding how to live out the practical suggestions—the emphasis is on your sexual identity. Its focus is to help you live your life faithfully before God as you continue to experience some degree of same-sex attraction.

The next two chapters provide a theoretical and theological foundation for the remainder of the book. In Chapter 2, you will read about what it means to affirm your sexuality, that sexuality is an intended part of God's good creation, and, of course, what this means to a person contending with same-sex attraction. In Chapter 3, you will read about several myths and discover what is true about sexuality and experiences of same-sex attraction.

The central chapters help you walk through a practical way of living your life. You learn to *recognize patterns in your life*, *plan your environment*, *trade in old scripts you've been living by for new ones*, and *live out a practical theology of sanctification*. Each chapter is intended to educate you about your experiences of same-sex attraction and behavior. This involves tracking patterns of same-sex attraction and learning how these experiences of attraction are related to thoughts, physical sensations, and acting out behaviors.

The goals of this book, then, include increasing your understanding of the things that influence your thoughts and behavior, enhancing competencies, identifying patterns of thinking and behaving, and utilizing various religious resources to help you live your life consistent with your understanding of God's call on your life.

The final three chapters are closing words for families, the church, and the person struggling with same-sex attraction. These are words to challenge and encourage the Body of Christ to identify and serve the image of God in all persons.

Reflections on Sexual Identity:

1. What would help you know whether the approach presented is a good fit for you? How can you begin to answer that question for yourself so that you are in a position to make truly informed decisions about your life?
2. Think back to the model of sexual identity development . In what ways does the model fit your experiences? In what ways do your experiences differ from the model? Which stage do you see yourself in when you read about the model?
3. Is it possible that your sexuality has a pre-existing claim upon it? If not, why not? If so, describe this pre-existing claim. Where does it come from? What claim(s) is it making? How do you know?
4. Reflect upon what it means to sustain resolve in your life. How do the factors mentioned (amount of same-sex attraction, experience in same-sex relationships, motivations, meaning making, and family and peer group support) fit with your interest in sustaining resolve? Are there other factors besides those mentioned above that you believe might help sustain resolve?

Chapter

2

Our Sexuality

Perhaps you have heard people say that sexuality is a "gift from God." This kind of statement can be confusing to Christians who contend with same-sex attraction and believe that homosexual behavior is wrong. Often these folks are active in a local church community that teaches that homosexuality is a sin, have tried for years to change their sexual orientation, and continue to contend with same-sex attraction. Although we believe our sexuality *is* a gift from God, we think this is something a person who contends with same-sex attraction wrestles with and comes to experience for themselves only over time. It is not a trivial matter that can just be summed up in a phrase or sound bite without causing a great deal of pain and confusion.

Several years ago, a Christian man entered counseling expressing concerns about his experiences of same-sex attraction. He had always been single and believed his sexuality was a curse. He had experienced same-sex attractions since his early teen years and wanted so badly to have them go away and be replaced by opposite-sex attractions so that he could enjoy a sexual relationship with a woman. When he heard well-intentioned friends from church refer to human sexuality as a "gift from God," he became indignant and further isolated because of his own experiences of attraction and the deeper, more penetrating experience of shame. It took several months for him to reach the conclusion that his sexuality was a stage upon which God was directing a complex drama about vocation (calling) and sanctification (being set apart for God's purposes). It was only then that he could share that he believed his sexuality was a gift from God, but not in the way most people commonly think. His sexuality was the primary place in his life where God worked out His redemptive plan, where God shaped and reshaped this man's priorities and values so that they more closely approximated God's priorities and values.

Lets take a step back and clarify what this man meant when he said he felt his sexuality was becoming a stage for God to work, or that his sexuality related to his experience of God's calling and sanctification. We affirm the view that sexuality is an important part of what it means to be human, but our sexuality also reflects our fallen condition. It is part of who we are as a person, and it so often stands in rebellion to what God wants for us. Just as in any other area of our lives, God works to bring about Christ-likeness. God has a plan that is greater than any one person, a greater plan than any one person's desire for pleasure through genital sexual activity. A person may not see it now or have the ability to see the future. Christians walk based on faith in Him. Following His word, trusting in Him, and having faith in Him, we can see that any one struggle is not the whole picture. God and His purposes are the big picture. Christians are called to allow themselves to be open to His purposes and calling on their lives. It should come as no surprise that God has a plan and purpose for your life here—in light of your experiences of same-sex attraction.

But isn't this book about how to help people change their sexual orientation? Why didn't the man mentioned above experience this more profound change—the disappearance of all same-sex attraction? The answer to the first question is that this book is not about changing sexual orientation; it is a book about living with experiences of same-sex attraction that have not yet changed despite one's best efforts. The answer to the second question—why didn't the man experience this more profound change—is that we don't know. Some people appear to experience change, while many others do not. But we wouldn't want to underestimate the profound change that he *did* experience. He experienced a life-changing reconsideration of how he looked at his sexuality. He began to experience his sexuality vocationally (as reflecting a more profound calling, rather than a curse) and through the lenses of sanctification, as a gift from God, through which He would work out His purposes.

Sometimes this vocation is lived out as a testimony. To the extent that a person feels called to share their story with others, their experience of vocation is one of testifying to God's work in their life—that through the person's experience of same-sex attraction, that person has learned more about God's love for them, and God's righteousness. That through their struggle they learned more about God's grace and mercy, about forgiveness and about what it means to be courageous. In fact, it was C. S. Lewis who noted that courage is central to living a virtuous life:

> Courage is not simply one of the virtues, but the form of every virtue at the testing point, which means, at the point of highest reality. A chastity or honesty or mercy which yields to danger will be chaste or honest or merciful only on conditions. Pilate was merciful till it became risky.[1]

Of course, most people who contend with same-sex attraction do so in anonymity. They do not share a public testimony of the work God is performing in them because the church oftentimes is not a place able to hear that particular struggle, unless it is an unqualified success story. And this kind of private vocation can be just as difficult to sustain. Public vocation and testimony can put pressure on a person to never backslide, and this pressure can lead to compromising behaviors to cope with that pressure. Private vocation can be more isolating and prone to relapse for other reasons, including a lack of social support and accountability.

The man mentioned above experienced his sexuality vocationally and in a private way. He is not a ministry leader nor does he offer a public testimony of his struggle or courage. But he has begun to surround himself with a small group of close friends who hold him accountable and who know that his courage runs a little deeper than most other Christians.

What often happens in the local Christian community is that people contending with same-sex attraction live in isolation from others. They struggle secretly with their same-sex attractions, feeling as though they have no one to openly talk with about their "signature" struggles.[2] What we mean by this is that everyone has a unique cluster of struggles with sin that varies from person to person, and those struggles shape much of the Christian life, as they set the stage for how God works through their life to make them more Christ-like.

You may be thinking that the isolation we are describing is endemic to the church and that no one really has other close Christian friends with whom they can share real struggles. There is a kernel of truth to this in some Christian circles. However, many people find their local church to be a place where they can admit to certain struggles, but not others. Unfortunately, churches often rank order moral concerns, and the church community can send messages about which sins are more tolerable for community life. For example, it is generally acceptable in most conservative churches to admit that you struggle with self-centeredness, pride, or impatience. There are fewer churches where a person can admit to difficulties with an addiction. But many churches will sponsor AA groups and have at least some association with people contending with addiction or substance abuse. But there are even fewer churches where a person can honestly admit to experiencing same-sex attraction.

What happens to the person who shares his or her struggles in a church community that is not mature enough to respond pastorally to these struggles? In our experience that person often writes off that local church and often the entire community of believers as being hypocritical. And they would not be far off the mark for doing so. Although there are communities of believers who have a vision for helping people live faithfully and with integrity with their sexual struggles, they are few and far between. Do you remember the old adage, "Don't throw the baby out with the bath water"? Yes, there are problems in the church, and there are people who, out of their own insecurities and signature struggles, behave in hypocritical ways, but there are also pockets of safe, supportive communities committed to the spiritual journey and maturity of its members. We will say more about this in Chapters 8 and 9 where we offer suggestions to family members and the church community on how they might be the Body of Christ in response to someone contending with same-sex attraction.

We turn our attention now to one of our great gifts and greatest vulnerabilities: our sexuality. The gift of human sexuality lies in part in the constant reflection of our desire to be connected to and completed by another. One expression of this desire for intimacy and connection is found in genital sexual activity, but it is not the only expression of that desire. Many people relate to close friends and family members and delight in others and the complimentary expression of their humanity without engaging in sexual activity with them.

Recently the question came up, "Will there be marriage in heaven?" This is an important question and one that is germane to our discussion because the answer is so obvious: Yes, but not marriage between people who are married here on Earth. There will be marriage in heaven because the Bride of Christ, the Church, will be married to Christ. All Christians, single and married alike, those contending with same-sex attraction and those who do not, will be married and fully completed by another, by Christ.

The gift also represents an opportunity to follow God in faithful obedience to His desire for us in how we image Christ in our lives. In this sense the gift is one of our great vulnerabilities, because the People of God have always faced the challenge of relating to God on His terms or on our terms. This is actually a question of idolatry, of "giving anything the worship and service that belong to God alone."[3] This includes our sexual attractions. This does not mean that people worship their sexual attraction; it means some people may struggle with living their lives in service to their sexual attractions rather than in service to God. This is a theme we will consider again at the close of this chapter.

We turn now to a Christian view of human sexuality. It can be difficult for people to integrate Christian ethics and sexual behavior in a culture that elevates sexual behavior as much as ours does. This is especially true when a person's sexuality unfolds in a way that makes it challenging to obey the traditional Christian sexual ethic with respect to God's revealed will for sexual behavior. In our permissive society it is accepted to satisfy or seek satisfaction of our sexual desires without giving thought to God's original intent for sexual behavior. But what is God's revealed will for sexual behavior?

A Christian Perspective on Sexuality

To begin, there is no explicit theology of human sexuality laid out neatly in the Bible. As much as we like to view Scripture as a manual we can turn to to tell us directly whether or not to engage in a specific act, it is not. We do find specific sexual acts condemned in Scripture; these include fornication (intercourse with someone who is not your spouse), incest, rape, sodomy, and lust. Other acts are explicitly affirmed: intercourse in marriage and celibacy outside of marriage. Still, many acts simply are not addressed directly: masturbation, oral sex, petting, and nudity. We do discover, however, a reasonably explicit set of ethical guidelines on the broader topic of human sexuality, and these guidelines can help us think through Christian sexual ethics and sexual behavior. This means that throughout Scripture we find an explicit design for how we should live faithfully before God in relation to sexuality and other areas of our lives. These guidelines can be organized around the four acts of the biblical drama[4]: creation, fall, redemption, and glorification.

We look in the book of Genesis and see that God created two sexes: male and female. Humanity is the pinnacle of God's creation, and God reflected on His creation, on the man and woman, and declared them "good." So in the Old Testament we see that God establishes marriage as between one man and one woman; they are now "one flesh." We see a corresponding affirmation of the creation account in the New Testament, specifically when Jesus responded to a question about divorce. Jesus admitted that God allowed divorce at the time of Moses because people are "hard-hearted," but it is certainly not God's intention that people divorce; it is not God's desire. In his response, Jesus references creation and reminds us that God brought man and woman together to delight in a union that would include the expression of their sexual attraction for one another. This general tone that speaks to the goodness of creation and a positive view of human sexuality is picked up in the Old Testament in the Song of Songs (see chapter 4:1-15), in the New Testament in Paul's letter to the church in Ephesus (Ephesians 5), and elsewhere in Scripture.

Christians also understand that we are all fallen creatures. Although we bear the image of God, we are tainted by the fall, and all aspects of who we are and of this world reflect this fallen condition. So it should come as no surprise that our sexuality, which was originally a good of creation, is in some way affected by the fall.

Put differently, each of us struggles with unique expressions of our fallenness, and it should come as no surprise that human sexuality is often the stage on which many of us express the drama of our fallen nature. And there are many ways in which our sexuality is affected by the fall. There is strife in male-female relationships that had not been there prior to the fall. There is also a newfound tendency to seek short-term gratification and to fragment others in such a way that we can now relate to them as mere objects for our own interests. People become objects to use for our own delight instead of people created in the image of God to be respected and valued. There is also a general rebellion as a motivating force in our lives, especially rebellion against God and other authorities.

At a concrete and specific level, many people report struggling with the effects of the fall in experiences of lust. For most people this involves lusting after those of the opposite sex; for some, this involves experiencing same-sex attractions. From the perspective of the traditional Christian sexual ethic, same-sex attraction is simply an expression of the fall, and viewing it that way seems to place it in a more accurate context in relation to other expressions of who we are as fallen creatures (see 1 Corinthians 5:9-13; 6:9-20; 7:1-9; Matthew 5:27-28).

But God does not leave humanity in our fallen condition. A proper understanding of redemption and glorification is essential to understanding this book. Scripture reminds us that God does not abandon us in our fallen state. Rather, He steps into our fallen world through the incarnation, through the person of Jesus, and He fully intends to redeem believers, to sanctify or make them holy, to set them apart for His purposes.

So we want to see our sexuality in the context of God's redemptive plan. Whether or not a person contends with same-sex attractions, many people contend with other issues that make sexuality difficult for them. Some struggle with sexual addiction. Others struggle with pornography. Still others struggle to take delight in their sexual relationship with their spouse. Each of these are expressions of how our sexuality is not what God intends for us. They are expressions of our fallenness. Again, in many respects, experiencing same-sex attractions should not be viewed as any worse than struggling with heterosexual lust, sexual addiction, or Internet pornography.

In addition to understanding a Christian view of human sexuality through the four acts of the biblical drama, it is important to point out issues that complicate our understanding of human sexuality and sexual behavior. These include our gender as male and female, our inherent physicality, what we mean when we refer to "the flesh," and the role of sexual identity in the expression of idolatry.

Gender

God created humanity as male and female, and our maleness and femaleness and experience of relationality were deemed good. Man was good. Woman was good. Together they are good. But single they are good too.

A woman we knew felt neutered, neither male nor female. She had sexual attractions for females, and she did not think of herself as a woman. In fact, due to all of the abuse in her home, when she was little she thought maybe it would have been better to have been born a boy. She really did not want to be a boy, but being a girl was not that great. In a ministry she was instructed to do girl things and helped with clothing, make-up, hair styling, and so on. The last straw for her was when one lady suggested she speak to a style consultant. The style consultant's suggestions came down to this: "avoid wearing pants for one year, and try and go without underwear a few days a week...this will help you feel more feminine and in touch with your body." Although the woman tried all of these suggestions, she still did not feel it was "good" to be a female. She continued to pray about this and surrender this to God. Finally, shopping with a friend at a local thrift store, she was hit with an overwhelming sense of herself as a "girl." She yelled across the clothing aisle to her friend "I'm a girl, and it's a good thing." This simple yet profound statement began a landslide of activity in her perceptions of herself. She went around for weeks telling people that God created her a girl and it was a good thing.

Although it is difficult to say how to cultivate this internal sense of oneself as male or female, it seems important that you come to terms with your sex (male or female), with your gender (masculine or feminine), and that these are two different yet complimentary expressions of the highest form of God's creation—that they are "good," and good in a complimentary way in the context of marriage where genital sexual activity takes place, "good" in platonic relationships outside of marriage where personality and temperamental difference are complimentary, and "good" in God's sight on their own merits.

Inherent Physicality

Scripture speaks of our inherent physicality.[5] That is, we are physical, sexual creatures by design, and our status as physical creatures is God's intention and a good of creation. This may seem obvious to you. You could not read the book you are holding in your hands without your hands to hold it up, your eyesight, and so on. We are more than souls; we are body and soul. However, if you are honest with yourself, you may admit that you struggle with whether this body of yours is a "good" of creation. It breaks down, gets injured, and we act on our desires through our bodies, engaging in all kinds of behaviors we later regret. So we may have mixed feelings about our bodies as "good." We may struggle with whether our physical bodies are somehow inferior to the soul or spirit God gave us, and we may desire instead a union with Christ that we secretly suspect will take place spiritually and have little if anything to do with our physical bodies. In other words, some people desire to separate their spiritual selves from their bodily selves, by placing greater emphasis on spirituality, when in fact the spiritual and physical are connected and physical bodies have a role in God's redemptive plan. We want to re-affirm God's plan to create us with physical bodies; that we are inherently physical, and that this physicality is good from God's perspective. We see this most clearly in creation, the incarnation, and glorification, so we will look at these three events more closely.

In the creation story we are told that God makes Adam from the earth. That He fashions a body and then breaths His spirit into him. In other words, we are physical creatures who receive God's life-giving breath. It is by God's design that we are physical. In fact, we are inherently physical. Again, God reflected on His creation and declared it "good."

The incarnation—that is, the fact that Jesus, who is God, became a man—re-affirms the goodness of the physical world. Jesus took the form of a man and ate, drank, slept, worked with his hands, and so on, just as we do. How could God become something that was inherently bad? The answer is that He could not. So we must conclude that Jesus became human, that He had an actual, physical body, and that having a physical body is a good thing in and of itself.

Finally, our future hope of glorification in heaven speaks to the goodness of our physical bodies. We are told that we will have a "new body" in heaven, and so there is something about what it means to be human that—by design—entails us having bodies, so much so that we have them here on this earth, and we will have them in the glory that awaits us.

The Flesh

Perhaps the greatest challenge to our understanding of the goodness of our physical bodies are the references in Scripture to the flesh. For example, in Galatians 5:19-21, we are told to resist the flesh of this world:

> Now the works of the flesh are evident, which are: adultery, fornication, uncleanness, lewdness, idolatry, sorcery, hatred, contentions, jealousies, outbursts of wrath, selfish ambitions, dissensions, revelries, and the life; of which I tell you beforehand, just as I also told you in time past, that those who practice such things will not inherit the kingdom of God.

Many Christians simply assume that the word "flesh" here refers to our physical bodies. The world "flesh" can mean the body in some contexts, but in Galatians we clearly see a list of sins that are far-reaching in their expression. Take a few minutes to read over the list. These are not all sins that have a physical basis. So it is impossible for "flesh" in this context to mean our physical bodies. Another meaning of the word "flesh" is our rebelliousness in relation to God. If we read Galatians 5 and think of putting aside our rebelliousness, the list really makes sense. This is the flesh we have to resist, not our physical bodies as such.

Idolatry

A final important consideration we see in Scripture is God's concern over our tendency toward idolatry. Richard Lints[6] recently wrote a paper on the relationship between idolatry and the image of God, and we will summarize some of his points as we make applications to the person who contends with same-sex attraction. Idolatry is really an in-house discussion among Christians. In Scripture, concern expressed over idolatry is aimed directly at Israel, God's chosen people, rather than other nations. God reacted to the idolatry of His people, as they were prone to turn away from Him and toward other gods. Idolatry, if it were to be distilled into its purest form, is really about subverting your relationship with God.

We want to return to the topic of idolatry in a moment, but at present we wish to distinguish three levels of understanding same-sex attraction. At the *first* level, the most descriptive level, some people experience same-sex attraction. It does not necessarily mean anything more than that: it is an experience that they have, and some people experience opposite sex attractions, while others report experiencing both same- and opposite-sex attractions. As we will indicate throughout this book, our experience is that this is the most accurate and helpful level of explanation and meaning-making for most people who experience homosexual attraction. For example, if Joe experiences same-sex attraction, it is more accurate and more helpful for him to say of himself, "I am a man who also experiences same-sex attraction," rather than to say of himself, "I am gay." The latter suggests he is a male and that his identity rests not in his gender but in his experiences of same-sex attraction. It also suggests something about same-sex behavior being a normal expression of who he is as a person. The first way of describing himself, that is, to say, "I am a man who also experiences same-sex attraction," is merely descriptive, and it says nothing implicit about what the experiences of same-sex attraction means and what moral conclusions can be drawn from acting upon the attractions.

The *second* level of explanation and meaning-making reflects consistent, persistent directionality of same-sex attractions. We commonly refer to such directionality of same-sex attraction as a homosexual orientation. For these people their attractions reflect a distinct preference; they reflect the directionality of their sexual preferences. For example, if Joe has been sexually attracted to men exclusively since his early teens years, does not report any current sexual attractions to females, and his attraction to males are frequent and reasonably intense, it may be accurate to say that Joe has a "homosexual orientation." Joe experiences same-sex attraction to such an extent and in such a way that he can accurately describe the directionality of his attractions as "homosexual."

At a *third* level are those who integrate their experiences of same-sex attraction into a "gay" identity. That is, they speak of themselves with respect to a self-defining attribution, "I am gay," and this identity implicitly communicates something about how they view same-sex behavior, most often as a natural expression of who they are as a person. For example, Joe could integrate his experiences of same-sex attraction into a "gay" identity.

In contrast to the person who experiences same-sex attraction or who has a homosexual orientation—for whom same-sex behavior is still under moral scrutiny—Joe could integrate his experiences into a "gay" identity, which carries with it the connotation that he celebrates same-sex behavior as a moral good, a natural extension of what it means to experience his sexual self-actualization in relation to himself and to others.

We now return to the issue of idolatry. For Christians who affirm the traditional Christian sexual ethic, that is, God's intention for sexual expression is in the context of marriage between one man and one woman and chastity for all, we believe that descriptive language provides you with the most latitude in how you shape and re-shape your sexual identity and worship God on His terms rather than your own (we will develop more of what we mean by "shaping" and "reshaping" sexual identity in Chapter 6). But it is important to understand that staying descriptive and saying of yourself, "I am a woman who experiences same-sex attraction," or "I am male and I also experience same-sex attraction," provides you with more freedom to think rather broadly about your sexual identity. By not integrating your experiences of same-sex attraction into a gay, lesbian, or bisexual identity, you say nothing concerning what you believe about same-sex behavior. You do not foreclose prematurely on your sexual identity and the broader question of who you are as a person. And this can be something you develop for yourself, believe privately, and share publicly to the extent you choose which is best for you. Even for those who experience persistent same-sex attractions and would say that they experience a homosexual orientation, there remains a kind of freedom to worship God on His terms, as we understand them, within a traditional Christian sexual ethic.

At this third level of integrating experiences of same-sex attraction into a "gay" identity, it seems inescapable that such persons are placing their identity as gay primary and that they then relate to God on these terms. It is not a failure to relate to God; people who take on a "gay" identity may very well relate to God, but the question is: *on whose terms*? We become who or what we worship, but the terms of agreement also shape our experience and outcome of worship. As Lints observes, "It is not merely 'giving yourself away' that is at stake in proper worship, but also 'whom you are giving yourself away to and in what manner are you giving yourself up.'"[7] Citing Martin Buber, Lints reminds us that we can worship God idolatrously, that is, "as an object for one's own purposes."

And so we have great empathy for the Christian who takes on a "gay" identity and worships God on those terms, but we are concerned about what may be gained at the expense of what may be lost. Our concern is that these Christians may have foreclosed prematurely on other options with respect to their sexual identity, their identity in Christ, and their relationship to God. We are asking, "What are the tradeoffs in Christians worshipping God on the terms set by themselves having integrated their experiences of same-sex attraction into a 'gay' identity?" Proper identity is found in the context of obedience to God's call on our lives.

We return to the idea that our sexuality is indeed a gift from God. Even if your sexuality—by no fault of your own—is directed toward members of the same sex, it is a gift from God because in all of our life experience and conditions, we have the opportunity to secure a vocation, a calling to live beyond our immediate interests and with reference to God's intention for human sexuality. In doing so we live out a practical theology of sanctification, of becoming more and more in the image and likeness of Christ.

Concluding Thoughts

As we draw this chapter to a close, we want to note that the themes that emerge from Scripture with reference to a Christian sexual ethic are often described as a *traditional* Christian sexual ethic. We used this language in this chapter, and continue to use it throughout this book. The book is intended for those who affirm the traditional Christian sexual ethic, struggle with same-sex attractions, and wish to live faithfully before God as they understand His revealed will for human sexuality. But a more accurate term would actually be a prophetic Christian sexual ethic, because the prophetic role we take is to constantly critique tradition so that we can affirm what is true about a Christian view of sexuality and sexual ethics, while rejecting claims that are false, even if those claims arise from Christian tradition. In other words, tradition is no guarantor of accuracy. But we do well to be cautious and conservative in moving away from a traditional Christian sexual ethic, to pronounce judgment on tradition, particularly in matters of what the church has taught to be of concern in the moral sphere. These are not matters of mere opinion but of eternal significance for the church and for those who earnestly desire to understand and follow God's revealed will as it pertains to human sexuality and sexual behavior.

Reflections on Your Sexuality:

1. How have you typically responded when people talk about sexuality being "a gift from God?" How have your experiences of same-sex attraction made that statement especially difficult for you? As you reflect on the main themes from this chapter, is there a part of you that can hold out the possibility that your sexuality *is* a gift from God, but not in the way you might have commonly understood the word, "gift"? How so?
2. Review in your mind the four acts of the biblical drama: creation, fall, redemption, and glorification. In what ways does organizing a prophetic Christian sexuality with reference to each of these four acts help you in light of your present struggles?
3. What does it mean to you to be male or female, masculine or feminine? What kinds of experiences have you had that complicate this area for you? How important is this to your sense of who you are as a person?
4. What do you think of the idea that we are inherently physical? If you agree with this assertion, what are the practical implications for you on a day-to-day basis? What does your inherent physicality have to do with your sexuality?
5. How does reading about "the flesh" as humanity's tendency to rebel against God's will change how you view your body and your present struggles? For some people this "levels the playing field" when it comes to discussions of sin. That is, rather than rank ordering sins and feeling as though homosexual behavior is especially bad, many people find it helpful to see where Scripture puts such behaviors side by side with other sins that many more people struggle with on a daily basis.
6. Do you believe that God can be worshipped idolatrously? How might this be done? How is it helpful to you to distinguish among three "levels" of meaning-making: experiences of same-sex attraction, a homosexual orientation, and a "gay" identity?

Chapter

3

Myth and Reality about Same-Sex Attraction

Many people today believe that homosexuality is a watershed issue for the church and broader culture. It is viewed as important for a variety of reasons, not the least of which are Christians' views of the authority of Scripture and its relevance today, the claims of the gospel on the life of the Christian, and one's personal experience of sanctification. So there is actually much at stake in the current debates, and this makes accurate information about homosexuality a premium.

Unfortunately, the discussions and debates about homosexuality can become confusing because there are many myths about same-sex attraction and behavior, and few people who know enough about the topic are willing to discuss it in an even-handed fashion. In this chapter we consider many myths and truths about homosexuality and same-sex attraction. As we work toward a shared understanding of what we know and do not know about homosexuality, take a minute to answer the following ten questions:

True	False	
☐	☐	1. Homosexual persons make up about 10% of the general population.
☐	☐	2. Homosexuality and experiences of same-sex attraction are caused by a person's homosexual gene.
☐	☐	3. Homosexuality is considered a mental illness by the major mental health organizations.
☐	☐	4. If a person tries hard enough, he or she can change his or her sexual orientation.
☐	☐	5. Expressing oneself through sexual behavior is essential to human happiness and wholeness.

- ☐ ☐ 6. Dating or marriage will help a person rid themselves of unwanted same-sex attractions.
- ☐ ☐ 7. Most self-identifying gay men and lesbians have just as many sexual partners as heterosexual men and women.
- ☐ ☐ 8. The Bible must be outdated or translated incorrectly since segments of the church and society embrace homosexual attractions and behaviors as a legitimate sexual alternative.
- ☐ ☐ 9. There is a systematic approach to helping people change same-sex attractions that works for everyone.
- ☐ ☐ 10. Focusing principally on the goal of a chaste life over orientation change is a sign that the person has given up.

What we will do now is answer each of the above questions.

Homosexual Persons Constitute about 10% of the Population.

The answer to this question is *false*. We have actually seen this inflated figure inflated even further to 12–15%, or higher in some discussions. This is a remarkable distortion of what researchers believe to be true today. The 10% figure was made popular by research conducted by Alfred Kinsey and his colleagues. The truth is that Kinsey never really said that "10% of the population is gay," but he did say that about 10% of the sample he gathered information on experienced same-sex attraction over about a 3–4 year period of time. His sample, however, was not representative of the general population, and he over-represented people who would have been more likely to engage in same-sex behavior over a 3–4 year period (such as sex offenders and prison inmates).

More recent and much more accurate research puts the prevalence rate of homosexuality at about 2–3% percent of the population. If asked if a person experiences same-sex attraction (rather than identifies oneself as homosexual), these percentages rise to about 5% of the population. So there are fewer people out there who identify themselves as homosexual or who experience same-sex attraction than many people think. Also, there are more people out there who experience same-sex attraction than who identify themselves as homosexual.

There has also been some research comparing rural and suburban areas of the country with urban centers. The results showed higher percentages of persons identifying themselves as homosexual in urban settings than other settings. This may partially account for the ongoing myth that about 10% of the population is homosexual, simply because this may be closer to the truth in urban settings than in the rest of the country.

Homosexuality and Experiences of Same-Sex Attraction Are Caused by a Person's Homosexual Gene.

The answer to this question is *false*. Not long ago the reigning belief was that homosexuality was caused by disturbances in parent-child relationships. This theory has had mixed support in terms of research, but has largely been overlooked in favor of research on biology. Several highly publicized studies throughout the 1990s attempted to support the "biological hypothesis" that homosexuality is caused by genetic factors or prenatal hormonal influences. These studies received a tremendous amount of attention and have been instrumental in lobbying efforts by some organizations within the gay community.

Our own experience is that most people believe that either (a) people are born homosexual, or (b) people choose to be homosexual. On the one hand, some people believe that people who experience same-sex attractions are "born that way," that *something* happened at the level of biology that causes them to be "gay." On the other hand, there are those who believe that people choose homosexuality. Because these people reject the biological hypothesis (in terms of direct causes of homosexuality), they feel they must hold people accountable for their homosexuality, as though the person one day made the decision, "I think I'll have a homosexual orientation for the time being."

If one or the other approach describes you, we would urge you to reconsider how you are thinking about homosexuality and same-sex attraction. By setting up this complicated issue as a "zero-sum" game, you may feel forced to believe one thing (biology) if the other is shown to be unlikely in some people (environment), or vice versa. But the truth seems to reflect a complicated combination of these two positions. We have yet to work with anyone who chooses to experience a same-sex attraction or a homosexual orientation. For the most part, they either want to be rid of their attractions, or they want the church to change its teaching on the moral status of same-sex behavior. None of the people we have worked with report seeking out these same-sex attractions, and most would choose to be free from them if it were in their power.

Does acknowledging that people do not choose to experience same-sex attraction mean that biology "causes" homosexuality in the same way that we can point to differences in hair and eye color? No. The research conducted to date on genetic and prenatal hormonal factors is inconclusive. From a research standpoint, the biological hypothesis is in about as good shape as the environmental hypothesis, so there does not seem to be a compelling reason to choose one over the other. It is more accurate to think of a combination of factors, including, perhaps, biology as expressed in temperamental differences or personality differences, that by itself would not "cause" homosexuality, but might provide a push in that direction for some people. Environment may also play a role to differing degrees for different people. No two people who experience same-sex attraction have exactly the same story to tell.

One last thought before we take up the next myth. Does acknowledging that people do not choose to experience same-sex attraction justify same-sex behavior? Many people seem to think that if they admit that people do not choose experiences of same-sex attraction, they have to say that same-sex behavior is okay. But this does not follow logically. There are many experiences that people have that they do not choose. People contend with thoughts and fantasies and attractions that they did not choose to have, but they contend with them anyway. Christians have historically not then viewed these thoughts, fantasies, or attractions as good; rather, Christians have held to a sexual ethic that calls people to reign in their thoughts and fantasies and to refrain from acting on their attractions through behavior.

Homosexuality is Considered a Mental Illness by the Major Mental Health Organizations.

The answer to this question is *false*. In the mid 1970s the membership of the American Psychiatric Association voted to support their board in removing homosexuality from the official manual of mental disorders. Psychology and counseling associations affirmed this decision, and today homosexuality is not considered a mental illness by any of the major mental health organizations. However, some members of each of these organizations disagree with some of the official policy statements produced by their respective organizations.

Although homosexuality is not listed as a mental illness in the official manual of psychopathology, there has been research on whether those who

identify as gay or lesbian are at greater risk for psy
words, does such identification place a person at ri
For example, research suggests that men and wom
or lesbian are at greater risk for depression, anxiety,
tine dependence, substance abuse, and suicidal ideati
people view these findings as a reflection of what it is [illegible]
that does not support homosexual persons; however, at least one study was conducted in the Netherlands where there is a great deal of support for homosexual persons. So this may be an interesting area for further research, and it will be viewed as important to people making decisions about their identity and behavior, as well as to those identifying themselves as gay or lesbian and wanting to improve their quality of life.

If a Person Tries Hard Enough, He or She Can Change His or Her Sexual Orientation.

This statement is also *false*. It is important to understand that effort does not always predict success when it comes to a change of orientation. Many people try for years and invest emotionally and financially in a change program only to continue to experience same-sex attraction at least occasionally. They are often hurt when they come across Christians who tell them that they just haven't tried hard enough, or that they just don't have enough faith that God will heal them. This last issue deserves a little more attention. How ought Christians respond to the charge that lack of successful change is an indication of too little faith in God's healing power?

Although we believe that God can intervene in a person's life and miraculously act to change any concern, including a person's unwanted sexual orientation, in most cases God does not intervene in this way. As with most other besetting conditions, God can bring healing, but He often chooses not to. In each specific case we don't know why God allows a person to live with any one of a number of conditions, but we do know that God promises not to abandon us in our struggles. C.S. Lewis once remarked on this and said that we must be content with ignorance about the causes of homosexuality. He encouraged believers to focus more on the vocation or sense of calling that can be found in any condition or life circumstance.

We also need to mention that some people, if they are honest with themselves, will admit to conflicted and even insincere attempts to change. We have worked with men and women who have always kept their "options open," never giving up or truly repenting from ongoing patterns of

…avior. They often barter with God: "When you take away my desires …ompletely, I will stop engaging in this sexual behavior." So while motivation does not guarantee complete success, conflicted and insincere attempts to achieve or maintain chastity or to work on sexual identity or orientation almost certainly can undermine a person's efforts.

Expressing Oneself Through Sexual Behavior is Essential to Human Happiness and Wholeness.

This, too, is a *false* statement. Again, the Christian sexual ethic holds that genital sexual expression is reserved for a husband and wife in marriage. This suggests that there will be many people who, if they choose to live by that ethic, will not be engaging in genital sexual expression. Among these, there are far more single persons who experience opposite-sex attraction than there are persons who contend with same-sex attraction. Each single person, then, has the opportunity (and not just the hope of marriage) to experience full, human happiness and wholeness.

It is also interesting to note that there is no major theory of psychology that holds that genital sexual expression is a prerequisite for human happiness and wholeness. Having made these points, we do not want to in any way downplay the significance of our sexuality to who we are as created beings. But there are several levels of our sexuality, including our gender sexuality (as male and female sexes), our erotic sexuality (evidenced in our longing for connection and completion in relationship with others), and our genital sexuality (actual genital sexual activity).[2] Rather than focus narrowly or exclusively on genital sexual expression, it may be helpful to broaden your understanding of your sexuality and its expression, so that you do not foreclose prematurely on what it means to delight in and express your sexuality.

Dating or Marriage Will Help a Person Rid Themselves of Unwanted Same-Sex Attractions.

The answer to this question is also *false*. We believe that neither heterosexual dating nor marriage will "cure" anyone of homosexual attractions. We certainly discourage people from choosing to marry as a form of "treatment." This is not sound advice.

The fact is that some men and women are married or in committed dating relationships and also experience same-sex attraction and struggle with same-sex behavior. The fact that they married or are dating does not lead to the end of their struggles, though it may have provided a sexual outlet, which can be important, particularly if a person experiences a mixture of same- and opposite-sex attractions (in contrast to the person who experiences only same-sex attractions).

How can this be? Doesn't the fulfillment of sexual intimacy within a heterosexual marriage eradicate all other desires? No, and this is apparent even if we were not discussing same-sex attractions. Marriage does not "cure" a person with opposite-sex attractions from experiencing attraction toward others who are not that person's spouse. We are reminded again and again that to be human is to be a fallen creature, and people experience the state of this fallenness in all areas of their lives, including their sexuality. Not only do persons in a committed dating relationship and marriage experience homosexual attractions, they also experience struggles with pornography, lust, heterosexual unfaithfulness, and various sexual addictions. Homosexual desire is one of a number of temptations with which the human mind and heart struggles.

A few years ago a married woman came to Lori distraught that her same-sex attractions had not gone away. Over the course of the conversation, she shared that since junior high she had experienced homosexual desires and engaged in two homosexual relationships. Following graduation, this young lady went to college and tried to distance herself from old friends and relationships. She met a young man and, after falling in love, decided to marry. During the course of their marriage, and much to her dismay, she began experiencing attractions for a female co-worker and subsequently began to struggle with same-sex sexual fantasies. Telling herself that she had everything under control, she neglected to talk to anyone about her desires. After a few months of struggling with intense sexual attractions, she entered into an adulterous affair. At the time of her consultation with Lori, this affair had been ongoing for just over a year.

Marriage is not a "treatment" for a person who contends with same-sex attraction. That does not mean that a person who experiences same-sex attraction cannot marry; but that decision should be made cautiously and always with open communication, openness to accountability, and a foundation of trust and intimacy.

Most Self-Identifying Gay Men and Lesbians Have Just as Many Sexual Partners as Heterosexual Men and Women.

The answer to this question is also *false*. Various studies have shown that on average people who self-identify as gay or lesbian have more sexual partners than heterosexual men and women. The largest sexuality study in the U.S. to date states that on average gay men report 42.8 lifetime sexual partners, compared to 16.5 for heterosexual men. On average lesbians report 9.4 lifetime sexual partners, as compared to 4.6 for heterosexual women.

Sexual monogamy or exclusivity has also been a point of discussion, particularly among gay males. In smaller, nonrepresentative samples of committed, stable gay couples, many if not all of those studied had had sexual encounters outside of the relationship. For example, in McWhirter and Mattison's study of 156 committed gay male couples, none of over 100 couples who had been together for over 5 years had been exclusive.[3] The researchers actually showed little concern for sexual non-monogamy, stating "...gay males expect mutual emotional dependability with their partner and that relationship fidelity transcends concerns about sexuality and exclusivity."[4] In other words, they make a distinction between emotional and sexual fidelity.

This does not mean that the next self-identifying gay male or lesbian you meet will be unable to maintain a monogamous or exclusive relationship. Some do, and they appear to be satisfied in those relationships. But the overall research suggests that self-identifying gay males and lesbians have a much higher rate of lifetime sexual partners and that non-monogamy is not uncommon, particularly in gay male relationships.

The Bible Must Be Outdated or Translated Incorrectly Since Segments of the Church and Society Embrace Homosexual Attractions and Behaviors as a Legitimate Sexual Alternative.

The answer to this question is also *false*. Many have attempted to convince themselves and others that the Bible has little to say about homosexuality and the verses that do prohibit this behavior are translated incorrectly, were meant for another "time and place," or do not speak to the kind of loving same-sex partnerships we see today. Using these arguments, segments of society and the church have begun to legitimize homosexual behavior through the ordination of sexually-active homosexual clergy, conducting same-sex unions, and legislating for change at the state and federal levels.

Lori recently talked with a woman about her desire to be accepted in her church community as a "Christian homosexual." She was frustrated that her church did not consider a lesbian identity a legitimate sexual alternative. She wanted her church to embrace her lesbian identity and celebrate her same-sex attractions. She gave two reasons for why her local church should change their views on the traditional Christian sexual ethic. First, there was a church in town that had two lesbian women as youth pastors. Second, the state of Vermont had legalized same-sex unions. This woman is not alone in her confusion about whether specific experiences should lead to radical changes in sexual ethics.

But the issue is really about whether Scripture affirms same-sex behavior as a moral good. Most scholars are in agreement that Scripture does not affirm same-sex behavior. Disagreements center on whether the church should change its understanding of the Christian sexual ethic, and sometimes this is placed alongside statements that the church has changed its views of women and slaves. Many churches today do not limit areas of responsibility for women; none endorses slavery. Though we cannot adequately address all of the issues in the current debates over interpretation of Scripture, we urge you to read resources, such as Robert Gagnon's book, *The Bible and Homosexual Behavior*,[5] an even-handed resource esteemed by conservative and liberal biblical scholars alike. Gagnon makes the compelling case that the whole of Scripture speaks to an openness to women and slaves not reflected in other cultures at the time of the writing. In other words, there was a progressive witness to changes that would set the nation of Israel, and then the early church, apart from other cultures. But this is exactly the opposite of what happens with respect to homosexuality. It would have been relatively easy to affirm homosexuality as such an affirmation would not have set the people of God apart from others. But Scripture's witness is to speak of homosexual behavior as immoral, to limit Christians with respect to this conduct, and it was this limiting and living within God's expressed will for sexual behavior that sets God's people apart from others.

There is a Systematic Approach to Helping People Change Same-Sex Attractions that Works for Everyone.

The answer to this question is also *false*. No one approach works for everyone, and not everyone will be helped by a particular approach. Contrary to popular belief, there are no systematic hoops to jump through to achieve "healing" from homosexuality. Each person is unique. As different as fingerprints, we each bring in humble petition to the throne of grace a multitude of interconnected experiences and actions that impact every area of our lives. The struggle with same-sex attraction will be similar in some ways, yet markedly different for each individual, as will the working toward your specific life goals.

Not having all the answers can be extremely frustrating. Walking into unknown territory and returning to some familiar places evokes fear and confusion. The unknown, wanting for someone to answer the questions, "What will happen next?" or "What do I have to do next?" may seem like the only thing to satisfy and calm the unrest within.

There was a young man, David, who battled this unrest for weeks, asking everyone he could, "How do I get rid of these feelings, what will work for me?" He kept their answers on a pad of paper by his bedside. Various ministries encouraged him to read certain books and attend groups for individuals struggling with same-sex attraction. Pastors and friends gave well-intended advice. His family wanted him to do *anything*—just do *something*. David was looking for the fastest and surest route to success.

It may be difficult to ask yourself this question, but, What *primarily* motivates you in your attempt to overcome same-sex attractions? Is it the pleas of a wife, a husband, or a family member? Is it to feel better, to remove shame and guilt? Or are you primarily motivated by a desire to have God define you, to have Him gently and masterfully remove all that is not of Him in you?

David is not unlike many who struggle with unwanted same-sex attractions and hope for the right answer, the perfect combination of steps to rid themselves of same-sex desires. But, there is none to be found. This sounds hopeless, yet it is a message of great hope. For in our uniqueness, God has a perfect plan to bring each one of us in perfect union with Himself. Some of the responses David received had no impact on his struggle, and some brought him closer to living faithfully before God. It is our hope that this book will be a resource to help you as you embrace God's work in your life and affirm the Christian understanding of God's standard of sexual purity.

Focusing Principally on the Goal of a Chaste Life over Orientation Change is a Sign that the Person Has Given Up.

The answer to our final question is also *false*. Giving up is turning away from God's goodness. Discontinuing concentrated efforts to explicitly change your orientation is not a sign that you are giving up. If your principal goal were chastity (with change of orientation as possible but not your focus), we would argue that chastity is a good state for single and married persons alike, and any movement towards God and His righteousness cannot be considered failure. Focusing less on changing your sexual orientation and more on living faithfully before God while still experiencing same-sex attractions is *not* the easy way out. It takes courage and commitment to acknowledge and squarely face sexual desires while affirming God's will for your sexuality and, whether attractions wane or not, to embrace living faithfully before God in the chaste state.

The journey of struggling with same-sex attractions is one of incredibly deep valleys and high mountains. We have heard this journey described as walking through the Valley of Baca, where weeping is common, and hope waits over the next rise. We do not want to hinder nor dissuade you on your path towards change, if that is what you choose. We do, however, want to encourage you by offering that chastity in the midst of the struggle with same-sex attraction is a lofty and worthy goal. It is a goal that chooses sexual purity and God's righteousness.

Reflections on Myths:

1. Read over the myths listed at the beginning of this chapter. Are there any listed that you had believed to be true? Identify some of the sources of misinformation? Do you see any themes among these sources?
2. How has buying into inaccurate and distorted information impacted you as you reflect on where you have been in your life and the life goals you are identifying for yourself today? How do you think misinformation makes it difficult for families or for the church to respond to persons struggling with same-sex attractions?
3. Are there other myths not included in this chapter that you personally have had to contend with? If so, what was the source of that particular misinformation?
4. What could be the benefits of educating society and the church about the myths related to homosexuality? How might you become a resource for education at some time in the future?

Part 2:

Managing Sexual Identity

Chapter

4

Recognizing Patterns

What are the habits that characterize your day? Some are quite innocuous: Do you drink coffee in the morning? Do you have a cup or two in the afternoon? Do you tend to wake up early? Do you go to bed late? Does the amount of sleep you get affect your ability to relate to others in constructive ways?

Other habits reflect patterns that may or may not impact sexual behavior: Do you tend to stop by a convenience store because you are attracted to the cashier? When you surf the Internet, do you participate in chat rooms where you discuss provocative sexual topics? Do you find yourself watching certain television shows for the people or the provocative storylines? Do you listen to certain music when feeling lonely or sad?

Patterns and habits can become so common that we may not notice them unless we intentionally reflect on our routine. The first step in our approach is to track specific patterns. Tracking patterns is important because without awareness of our behaviors, thoughts, or feelings, we have the potential to relate to others and go about our life in self-defeating and destructive ways. Starting with patterns and habits is a common practice in almost all efforts to help people with any number of concerns. The point is to get a sense for what is happening in your daily and weekly routine, simply because most people get into habits that would go unnoticed if not for an intentional effort on their part to recognize or take note of them.

Think about your ride to work. Say you have been driving the same route for the last four years and you get promoted, but your new position is in a different office across town. You drive to the end of your street, and instead of taking a left—your new route—you take a right. You realize you are going in the wrong direction. Habit. Turning to the right set you on the wrong course. Actions carried out without reflection set into motion consequences of varying significance.

Of particular importance to you are patterns of same-sex attraction and behavior. Now some people think that this is quite obvious: "Of course, I know better than most when I feel attractions to others. What's the point?" The point is that most people who are distressed by their experiences of same-sex physical and emotional attraction or sexual behavior often know little about their own daily and weekly routine and how different experiences increase the intensity, frequency, or duration of same-sex attraction. How often do you really sit down and ponder your sexual or emotional attractions? When was the last time you thought about the patterns of your sexual desires and how they ebb and flow throughout the week? Granted, this isn't something you discuss standing around the coffee machine at work, but imagine the implications of taking a step back and looking at your sexual and emotional attractions and sexual behaviors.

Let's consider a brief example. Sam was 32 when he entered therapy seeking help with his same-sex attractions and recent episodes of same-sex acting out behavior. He had no idea what circumstances facilitated his experiences of same-sex arousal or the intensity of the arousal on a day-to-day-basis. He also did not understand the influences in his life that led to his acting out through same-sex behavior during times of great emotional and interpersonal stress. So he worked for several weeks on tracking his experiences of same-sex attraction. Sam kept a journal, writing down his physical sensations, thoughts, and behaviors insofar as they related to same-sex attraction. For Sam these translated into predominantly physical sensations, such as an erection, sexual thoughts, thoughts intended to distract himself from acting on them, and feelings of both excitement and guilt. Our goal was to help Sam see the connections among the various dimensions to his attractions. The connections helped Sam predict the likelihood of his acting in ways that were consistent with his goals for counseling. When he found himself behaving in ways counter to his goals for counseling, we re-examined these patterns to further understand his difficulties.

As Sam's experiences indicate, the four major areas we want you to consider in this chapter are your physical sensations, thoughts, feelings, and behaviors. Sam recorded his experiences in a format similar to that found in Worksheet 4.1. Begin by listing the date and time of the event. Next, write out the situation shortly after it occurs—don't wait too long because your memory of the situation will fade, and you want to capture as much information about the experience as possible. Over the course of the next week or two, you might complete this worksheet for each particularly salient experience of same-sex attraction to give yourself a baseline (a starting point to which you can return to make comparisons as you track your experiences some weeks, months, or even years from now).

For example, Sam might write: "4/15 at 12:30 pm." He can then write down the *situation*: "I went to lunch with a couple of friends. A very attractive man was seated with a companion next to us." As he reflects on his *physical sensations*, he can write, "heart raced, felt flushed." He can also track his *thoughts*: "I want to sit with him; not sure I should." Sam can also track his *feelings*: "aroused, anxious, excited, guilty." Lastly, Sam can note what he did, or his *behaviors*: "Kept looking in his direction. I decreased interaction with my lunch companions. The man eventually left the restaurant; my eyes followed him out the door."

In the space that follows we unpack the meaning and practical application of each of the major areas: physical sensations, thoughts, feelings, and behaviors. We will also give you further examples and additional directions for completing your journal records.

Patterns of Response

Physical Sensations

There are many physical sensations associated with sexual attraction, including increased heart rate and perspiration, erection (in males), lubrication (in females), and so on. One of the many gender differences with respect to same-sex attraction is that awareness of physical sensations may be more obvious to men than women. Men often report specific physical changes, such as engorgement of the penis, which is what happens as they experience an erection—blood flows into the spongy chambers of the penis. They may also experience symptoms like sweaty palms, a racing heart, etc.

As you record your situations of sexual attraction and/or emotional longing, we encourage you to include a section on physical sensations. Individuals that we have counseled have found this particular element of the journal eye-opening and most helpful when attempting to make changes in their thoughts and behaviors. For this first part, we want to focus on physical sensations. It may be helpful for you, as you contend with same-sex attraction, to track your specific experiences.

Jeff was convinced he could never stop his "acting out" behaviors. According to Jeff, "it" would just happen. He would find himself in the park engaging in sexual activities before he knew what had happened. Recording physical sensations allowed Jeff to become more aware of his body and the people or situations that he found arousing. Jeff began to slow down the process, taking snapshots if you will. Over time, and based on his newfound awareness, Jeff made a number of changes in his thought processes and behaviors that were more consistent with his life goal of chastity.

Although women may also experience overt physical sensations, such as vaginal lubrication, racing heart, sweaty palms, and the like, they often report feeling more tuned into their sense of connection with others. This sense of connection is essentially feelings-based and emotional. And sometimes this is a more subtle change, one that may develop slowly in a close relationship with another woman.

Mandy, feeling trapped in a cycle of emotional dependence and sexual intimacy, wanted help identifying how she continually found herself in what she believed to be "destructive" relationships. Identifying physical sensations was extremely difficult for Mandy and something she avoided because of her abusive past. She had, in a sense, disconnected with this aspect of her self. Initially, Mandy could only explain her sensations as a compulsion to be alone with the individual, to have their complete attention. Through her commitment to understand this "compulsion" and her subsequent behaviors, Mandy systematically examined aspects of her desires and attractions.

We encourage you to begin to focus on and track your physical sensations. You can write them down as journal entries, utilizing the format in Worksheet 4.1. What physical sensations accompany your experiences of same-sex physical or emotional attraction? Again, these may include obvious things, such as penile engorgement or vaginal lubrication, or you may experience more subtle signals of sexual arousal that are particular to you, for example, sweaty palms, racing heart, and dizziness.

Sometimes, simply becoming aware of early signs of sexual arousal can help you decide whether you want to continue to think or relate or behave in ways that further contribute to sexual arousal or an intense emotional connection, or whether you would rather choose alternatives that are more in keeping with your goals in life.

Thoughts

Although physical sensations are an important indicator of sexual arousal, sometimes a person's accompanying thoughts and feelings play a critical role in what happens next. Let's further our understanding of this by considering your thoughts. You can begin to identify the thoughts that go through your mind as you experience same-sex attraction. Thoughts will vary significantly from person to person based upon any number of factors. You may be a young adult who has little, if any, sexual experience. Perhaps you are considering living a chaste life in response to your experiences of same-sex attraction. You may have a lot of fantasies about what same-sex behavior or a same-sex relationship could be for you. These fantasies may be especially challenging for you simply because chastity will rarely look as attractive as fantasies that carry with them all of your hopes and expectations for fulfilling sexual experiences.

Dreaming of a perfect relationship, Sarah spent a great deal of her time fantasizing about finding someone to love her. She played out scenario after scenario in her mind. She reworked a past relationship, changing hurtful remarks and filling empty promises. In the end, she was loved and adored. Sarah was determined to embrace the teachings of her faith, but found it difficult to let go of the "good things" in the relationship. Longing for companionship and acceptance, Sarah's mind was preoccupied with images and ideas of how things could be, in her words, "in another place and time." Sarah's thoughts influenced her feelings and her behaviors. The ideal was so much better than the reality, yet the ideal and her dependence on this imagined state was dictating her future.

Frank had no prior sexual experience, with the exception of kissing and light fondling. Yet, he had a high sex drive and reported frequent same-sex thoughts and fantasies. If you are like Frank you may find that your fantasy life is rather rich and developed, so much so that same-sex behaviors hold out the promise of being tremendously fulfilling. In fact, for Frank, chastity, which was his goal, was especially difficult because he had not found same-sex behavior to be disappointing, as some others had; he often compared his difficulties with celibacy to an exceptional fantasy life. In fact there was no comparison. His fantasy life won every time, unless he could begin to see and experience the rewards of living a chaste life in keeping with his religious beliefs and values about God's intentions for sexual thoughts and behavior.

Or perhaps you have had a number of sexual experiences or same-sex relationships. Perhaps you are in your twenties, thirties, or forties. You may be trying to live a chaste life after years of same-sex behavior. So your *thought* life may reflect your previous experiences. It may be more challenging for you to keep thoughts of prior sexual encounters, people, or scenarios in previous relationships out of your mind as you experience sexual arousal in present relationships. When you are not working on a project for your job or focused on a task at home or in the community, perhaps your thoughts stray to those sexual encounters or same-sex relationships, and you find them difficult to shake.

Mario Bergner, in his book, *Setting Love in Order*, describes himself as having this kind of history. He was trying to live faithfully before God following several years of same-sex behavior. He essentially says he threw himself into the gay lifestyle. His thought life reflected his previous history, and he writes about the challenges he faced in saying "no" to those thoughts and fantasies, so he could say "yes" to other things he felt God wanted for him. Mario also discussed his need to make changes in his environment, to pray over certain items, or about specific behaviors that had become symbolic of his struggles with homosexual attraction. This kind of environment management is important, and we will discuss it further in the next chapter.

At a most basic and descriptive level, Mario Bergner, and many others who contend with same-sex attraction, experience a number of conflicting thoughts. People are often torn in their desire to act on their urges and their intention to resist the urge to act out sexually. For example, one person may think, "That guy looks like he might be interested," while also thinking, "Stop this, you know you are not supposed to be thinking this way." Another person may think, "She seems like someone I could really connect with," while also thinking "...a friendship is fine, but I'm beginning to go down the path of fantasy..." Don't be surprised if you have conflicting thoughts. That's completely normal. This kind of ambivalence simply reflects your desires to connect with others, the fact that you experience same-sex attraction, and your beliefs and values that acting on these beliefs and values that acting on these thoughts through same-sex behavior would be immoral. In our experience it is simply better to be honest with yourself that you have ambivalent thoughts as opposed to denying or minimizing these thoughts.

Tracking thoughts also gives you greater insight into how specific thoughts may contribute to experiences of same-sex attraction. If you were to see someone you would normally find attractive and say to yourself, "Well, that's someone who looks good, but that's not what I'm going to be about," that would be quite a contrast to, "There's someone I could hook up with, and if he looks this way, that means he's interested." So sometimes thoughts play a role in encouraging acting out behavior.

A common way to think about your thought life is to imagine your thoughts as "tapes" that run in your head. What are the current tapes you hear? Where did these tapes come from? By tracking thoughts, you can begin to discover alternatives to the tapes that are currently running. Some people actually visualize themselves hitting the "stop" button on the tape player in their mind, and then they "eject" the tape they're hearing. What seems to be effective is to then replace that tape with another tape that reflects thoughts conducive to facilitating your life goals.

Examples of conducive thought tapes vary. What seems important, though, is to develop patterns in your thinking specific to your needs and personality. One young woman reported utilizing a visualization of tossing water on fiery darts. She conceptualized the fiery darts as negative thoughts about herself or sexual thoughts about another. Another individual reported utilizing the following statement, "Jesus, the Hope of Glory within me," to help monitor their thought processes. From reciting prayers and Scriptures to visualizing various life-sustaining images, we have counseled individuals who report a substantial change in both their attitudes and thoughts.

You do not have to live at the mercy of destructive patterns in your thinking. You can instead choose to explore and implement healthier thinking patterns. Returning to Worksheet 4.1, record your thoughts as they relate to sexual attraction and emotional longing. As you did previously, record the date/time, the situation, and physical sensations. Now we encourage you to add a section for your thoughts, and do not forget to acknowledge conflicting thoughts, as these are not uncommon.

Feelings

Thoughts and feelings are closely connected. How individuals *think* about their circumstances often contributes significantly to how they *feel* about their circumstances. For example, if you are pulled over for speeding, you might think, "I was only going seven or eight miles over the speed limit. Why didn't they give a ticket to that sports car that zoomed by a minute ago?" This could lead to feelings of frustration, anger, or resentment. In contrast, you might think, "Well, I was going over the speed limit, and I know better than that." This kind of thought would not fuel anger, though you may be somewhat frustrated with yourself for speeding and the fact that you were caught. But it does not fuel anger or resentment as such.

Let's apply this understanding of the connection between thoughts and feelings to tracking your experiences of same-sex attraction. If you recently experienced same-sex attraction while meeting someone at a conference or business trip, you could think to yourself, "What am I doing? This is absolutely unacceptable. I shouldn't keep struggling with this. What kind of a person am I?" These thoughts could lead to frustration, anger, guilt, and shame. These feelings may actually lead you to act out on your attractions, simply because people more often try to soothe themselves when they feel disconnected or out of control. This is what some people experience when they report negative emotions. These negative emotions can further fuel sexual attractions and lead to acting out behavior.

Beth entered the counseling session frustrated. She exclaimed, "Here we go again!" According to Beth, she experienced sexual thoughts about Robin, a new friend she had met a couple months ago. As she pulled out her worksheet, she commented on her skepticism about the process of recording her experiences. "What good is it going to do now!? The friendship is over; I can't even have a friend without thinking about sex!" Over the course of the next hour, Beth was able to put to paper the incident that had her so upset and ready to end her friendship with Robin. Exploring her thoughts and her subsequent feelings of shame, self-hatred, and frustration shed light on Beth's desire to end the relationship. It also facilitated a discussion of alternative responses she could make in her thinking and behaviors.

Contrast the reaction above with the following thoughts: "Well, these attractions certainly make sense. That's the kind of person I have often been drawn to emotionally. But I can choose what to do with these attractions. I can act on them, or I can say 'no' to them so I can say 'yes' to other things I want in my life." These thoughts do not deny or minimize a person's experiences of same-sex attraction; nor do they fuel experiences of guilt or shame, which would further fuel acting out behavior.

The following week Beth entered the counseling session with a wide grin glued to her face. Reframing feelings of sexual attractions for Robin as a "learning experience," Beth became somewhat of a junior detective. She reported sitting at dinner with Robin when images of being in an embrace with Robin began flooding her mind. She recorded the situation as follows: "I was having dinner with Robin, and we were talking about how we both love the winter season, with cozy dinners and sitting by the fireplace. *Physical Sensations*: I noticed feeling the physical sensation of warmth and an ache in my body. Image of holding Robin crossed my mind. *Thoughts*: I would love to hold her. This isn't about Robin; it's about longing to be loved; Robin is my friend. *Feelings*: sad, but also happy. Sad that I feel lonely, but happy that I can recognize my longing as okay."

Take a look back at your worksheet. We encourage you to practice recording your feelings, in addition to physical sensations and thoughts. Take a moment to think of a recent situation. Record it on a sheet of paper and then sit for a moment, focusing on the physical sensations you experienced.

Write those down. Now, record the accompanying thoughts, and finally your feelings. Hang on to this example. We will return to it once you have read the next section.

Behaviors

It may also be helpful to track your behaviors as you experience same-sex attraction. For example, one person may write about how he drove by a park where he used to be sexually active, and he may write down: "Driving by the park where last year I met someone." The same person may write down what he did with respect to his attractions: "I stopped the car and began to walk around." Or the person might write down what he did after the experience of same-sex attraction: "I called a friend and told her where I was; she encouraged me to drive to a coffee shop and meet her there."

Think about your behavior in its total context. An event takes place, and you experience physical sensations. You have thoughts about the event, followed by feelings about the event. This process is sustained by behaviors and culminates into some form of action. Imagine you are watching television, a romantic, sexually provocative movie, and you become sexually aroused.

Reflect on what led to the circumstances in which you were aroused. Let's back up and record this together. *Situation*: "After a lousy day at work, I picked up the TV guide and noticed a movie on cable with my favorite actress." *Physical Sensation*: "Tickling feeling in my chest." *Thoughts*: "I shouldn't watch this, it has some nude scenes; go ahead what could it hurt?" *Feelings*: "Excitement." *Behavior*: "Watched the movie."

You can also use the worksheet to track what you did as you were aroused. In the example we have been working with you might first track your response (*situation*): "I continued to watch the movie." *Physical sensation*: "My breathing became faster, my face flushed, a throbbing sensation in genitals." *Thoughts*: "Sexual images and the thought I better stop watching this. This can't be good for me." *Feelings*: "Excited, guilty." *Behavior*: "Watched the movie until it ended."

What did you do following the experience? A number of scenarios could come from this question, as could a number of scenarios from the previous experiences. Individuals are unique and respond in various ways to sexually arousing situations. How about you? What would you have done? Think about the situation for a moment. Can you imagine what physical sensations you would encounter? How about your thoughts or feelings? Can you predict your behavior?

Let's go back to the sheet of paper you set aside earlier. You have your situation recorded, the physical sensations you experienced, and your thoughts and feelings. Now, record your behaviors. What did you do? How did you respond? Ask yourself how you would respond differently if placed in that situation again, based on your awareness of the interaction between physical sensations, thoughts, feelings, and behaviors?

Again, you can use this worksheet anytime. We especially want to encourage you to be sure to use it in the beginning to give yourself a sense of the themes that emerge in the patterns characterizing your day-to-day life. The activity itself will be helpful to you, and it will provide you with much needed information of the kinds of activities that you may choose to avoid in order to facilitate your life goals. Of course, to make good use of these themes and patterns, you will want to reflect on how often they occur. Are they part of your daily routine? Can you track them over the course of several weeks or even months? Are you able to resist the urge to act on your attractions on a day-to-day basis, but is it more difficult over weeks and months, and can you begin to predict times that may be particularly hard for you? This is essentially another way to look at patterns.

Another Look at Patterns

So far we have been focusing on tracking patterns of physical sensations, thoughts, feelings, and behaviors. But there is another way to think about these and related patterns. We might also consider the length of these patterns. There are at least four distinct lengths worth considering: brief, here-and-now patterns, daily routines, weekly and monthly patterns, and generational patterns.[1]

Brief, Here-and-Now Patterns

The shortest patterns are those that happen throughout the day. We can think of these as brief, here-and-now patterns, but they also include the patterns of self-talk that people engage in every day. These patterns are hard to track, simply because there is a constant internal dialogue. But there is valuable information to be gained from slowing yourself down, attending to your thought life, and tracking patterns that revolve around the kinds of things you say to yourself about your attractions and behavior.

When you think about literal face-to-face exchanges (in contrast to internal dialogue), what are you saying to others, how are you relating to them? You can reflect on what you actually say about same-sex attractions and behavior, but you can also reflect on ways you relate to others that may contribute to your feeling disconnected from others. When these exchanges continue throughout a day or over the course of days or weeks, then you find that there is a cumulative effect to these patterns.

Let's look at some examples of brief, here-and-now interactions. Say you work for an overbearing boss who enjoys embarrassing his employees. You have a number of interactions with him wherein you feel belittled. You struggle with thoughts and feelings of rejection and inferiority, but you are afraid to confront him. After an interaction with him, you may begin to "rewrite" the situation in your mind through fantasy. Instead of dealing with the situation, you may begin to imagine yourself as in control, or better, you're the boss. You also may utilize fantasy to help you escape from your emotions, being someone else or somewhere else. Any one exchange with your boss can be frustrating, but the exchange can also come to characterize your daily routine, and this can lead to significant consequences over time. For now we want you to simply reflect on your brief, here-and-now patterns of behavior so that you can decide if you are relating and reacting to others in ways that support your life goals.

Daily Routines

The next patterns are our daily routines. These often result from a string of brief, here-and-now encounters, and they can also reflect your daily rhythms and routines as you get up, go to work, deal with co-workers, employers and employees, interact socially, spend time with your friends and family, and so on. You may feel that your daily routine is particularly fulfilling to you. Or, you may struggle with it. Perhaps each day is a new struggle as you find your energy depleted through very difficult exchanges at work or at home.

These patterns are a little easier to identify than face-to-face exchanges, but not as easy to see as weekly or monthly patterns. In other words you may be quite familiar with your daily routine, but you may have very little idea of how that routine fuels your need to soothe yourself, unwind, release tension, or find an outlet. Your daily routine is embedded in a longer pattern—your weekly and monthly routine.

Let's look again at the above example of the belittling boss. All day you have various meetings with him. You have been "checking out" frequently. You imagine yourself throwing a glass of water at him or firing him as you fantasize that you are the boss. On the way home, you drive by a fast food restaurant and get a burger because you "owe it to yourself." When you get home, you grab a glass of wine and "numb out" in front of the television wanting to put an end to the day. Before you go to bed, you play the song that reminds you of a previous same-sex relationship. While slipping into thoughts of a "lost love," you drift off to sleep. To your dismay, the alarm clock sounds too early, and you awaken with the events of the previous day unresolved.

Weekly and Monthly Patterns

Often overlooked sequences of behaviors are our weekly and monthly patterns. Whereas we may be somewhat familiar with our daily routines, few of us are familiar with how those routines are embedded in longer sequences that occur over a week or more. We mentioned above that weekly or monthly routines are easier to see than daily routines, but this may seem counter-intuitive to you. Let us qualify this point. It may actually be more difficult to identify many aspects of your weekly or monthly routine (as compared to your daily routine), but it is most typically your weekly or monthly routine that leads to acting out behavior that causes your distress. Not all weekly or monthly patterns are problems for you, but the problems you have are probably most easily seen as weekly or monthly patterns of behavior. For most people it is as though difficult exchanges with others or negative self-talk accumulates over the course of several days or weeks, and they find it increasingly difficult to resist the urge to engage in self-soothing behaviors. Now, many self-soothing behaviors (reading books, going for a stroll, working out, calling a friend) can be quite healthy. But often people will turn to self-soothing behaviors that run contrary to their life goals. Some may log onto the Internet and download homosexual pornography. Others may masturbate to same-sex fantasies or seek out a same-sex partner. These are "self-soothing" insofar as the person feels out of control or disconnected prior to the behavior and more in control or connected to others following the behavior.

Let's return to Sam and see how his weekly and monthly patterns led him to self-soothing behaviors that made reaching his life goals more difficult. Sam, who we mentioned earlier, has been in counseling for several months. He reports having a close relationship with his mother and a distant relationship with his father. He admits after several months of counseling that his close relationship with his mother is actually too close at times. At least he reports feeling criticized by her for his interests and hobbies, and he feels she shares her opinions on things like what he should wear, or the home he should live in. When asked about this, Sam denies any negative emotions toward his mother. Occasionally he will admit to some mild irritation, but he is not frustrated, resentful, or angry, by his account. Over the course of three or four months, however, Sam finds himself packing away these negative emotions. When he has a particularly difficult exchange with his mother he feels powerless to assert himself in their relationship, and he turns to sexual behaviors to manage his out of control feelings. His preferred sexual behavior is to seek out others through the Internet for a same-sex encounter of some kind. As a Christian, Sam reports that this is distressing to him. He reports wanting to live a chaste life. But he gives up the freedom to choose otherwise when he gets so wrapped up in his feelings of anger and resentment toward this mother, especially as these feelings go unexpressed in their relationship and only fuel his need to self-soothe.

Generational Patterns

The longest patterns are generational patterns. These are patterns of relating that are passed down through generations. These are almost as difficult to identify as brief, here-and-now patterns. Many of the other patterns of relating are embedded in a much longer sequence of behavior that is passed down from family to family. Probably the most effective way to examine these patterns is to work with a professional who is trained to reflect on your family in this way and work collaboratively with you to draw out possible themes for your consideration.

Essentially, you are reflecting upon how people in your family related to one another. How did they express anger? How did people in your family know when others were angry? What about affection? When you were growing up, how was affection expressed in your family? How did your family deal with modesty, nudity, and the like? When it came to sex education, were you properly educated about sexual anatomy and behavior, and were these issues discussed with reference to standards of right and wrong? If so, what were those standards? Did your parents live their lives in a manner consistent with the standards for moral conduct that they taught, or did they approach sexual ethics from the standpoint of "Do what I say, not what I do?"

We do not want to focus too much on your parents without expressing empathy for their experiences, too. Do you know anything about how they were raised? What was their family of origin like with respect to sexual education, messages about sexual ethics, and healthy boundaries for sexual behavior? Some people just do not know this information, and they do not have a relationship with either parent in order to explore this further. Others have the kind of relationship with either (or both) parents and are able to ask about what it was like to grow up in their family of origin. Sometimes valuable information is shared about what it meant to be a man or what it meant to be a woman. Your parents may have then drawn upon those messages (or reacted strongly *against* those messages) to raise and educate you.

But for most families these messages are hardly systematic and sometimes not even intentional. Families simply share and educate doing the best they can. And most families educate far more through modeling behavior and ways of relating and expressing anger and affection that are not part of an official "teaching" time for children. Simply by watching their parents relate to each other (or fail to relate in meaningful ways), children learn a great deal about intimacy, respect, trust, and so on.

It can be helpful to have you reflect upon these implicit and explicit messages about a range of attitudes and values that inevitably shaped your views on sexuality and sexual behavior. Laura's mom hated men. She was belittling towards her husband, and she taught Laura to never trust or rely on men. Laura described her father as a passive and weak man, and she was angry with her father that he didn't stand up to her mom. She never wanted to be like her mom, nor marry anyone like her dad. Laura's ideas about love, relationships, and gender roles were greatly influenced by her environment and the interactions within her family.

How can you use your understanding of brief, here-and-now patterns, daily routines, weekly or monthly patterns, and generational patterns to support your life goals? First, you may have already found it helpful just to reflect on the patterns of behavior. In doing so you may come up with themes that you would not have seen otherwise. You may begin making better choices in relating to your boss, your neighbors, your friends, or your family. Sometimes interrupting patterns of relating can help support your life goals.

Second, the themes you identify can be discussed with a close friend or accountability partner. It is important to have a person or a small group of people you can discuss your experiences with, and who will give you honest feedback. One place to begin is to consider a support group for those who struggle with sexuality-related concerns. Groups affiliated with Exodus International, Homosexuals Anonymous, or Courage, for example, provide support and accountability to many people around the world who struggle with homosexuality and other issues (see Appendix B).[2] If you do not live in an area in which you have access to such a group, you might consider an Internet-based support group (HA, for example, offers Internet support groups), and while perhaps not ideal, they at least provide encouragement and support.

Reflection on Patterns:

1. What are some of the more common physical sensations you experience when you feel sexual or emotional attraction toward others? Although these are most typically thought of as brief, here-and-now patterns of physical sensations, do you notice patterns at certain times of the day or week? When are you more likely to find yourself experiencing physical sensations of sexual or emotional attraction toward others?
2. Can you identify the tapes that tend to run in your head as you anticipate, experience, and consider acting on experiences of same-sex attraction? Are there times during a given day or week when you are more likely to hear tapes that are counterproductive to your life goals? Are there times when you have more success "ejecting" counterproductive tapes and replacing them with tapes that are consistent with you life goals?
3. What feelings do you associate with patterns of attraction? Have you ever made the distinction between *guilt* for specific behaviors and *shame* for feeling as if you are not a good person? What makes this a helpful distinction?
4. Do you see a connection between patterns of thinking and feeling and subsequent behaviors? Are there certain thoughts and feelings that take you down a path away from your life goals? Are there ways of thinking and feeling that take you down a path toward your life goals? Reflect on these in terms of brief, here-and-now exchanges, your daily routines, and longer patterns over the course of weeks or months.

Worksheet 4.1. Sexual Attraction/Emotional Longing Record

Date/Time	Situation

Physical Sensations	Thoughts	Feelings	Behaviors
1.________	1.________	1.________	1.________
________	________	________	________
________	________	________	________
2.________	2.________	2.________	2.________
________	________	________	________
________	________	________	________
3.________	3.________	3.________	3.________
________	________	________	________
________	________	________	________

Chapter

5

Environment Planning

One of the most amazing findings in the area of sexual behavior is that our environment contributes significantly to what we experience as sexual attraction as well as what manifests as a result of our attractions. This is surprising because we often think of sexuality as inherently biological, that Nature rather than Nurture directs our sexual behavior. There was a time in the 1990s when researchers were attempting to make the case that biology determines a homosexual orientation in the same way that biology determines eye color or hair color, and one of the more often-cited studies was actually of genetically altered fruit flies. The fruit flies—or Drosophila—were genetically altered to produce "homosexual" behavior. Some members of the gay community heralded this as evidence that biology rather than environment "causes" homosexuality. What was often omitted was the fact that when normal, non genetically altered fruit flies were introduced into the same habitat as the genetically altered fruit flies, the normal fruit flies engaged in the same "homosexual" behavior as the genetically altered flies.[1] We want to state that both Nature and Nurture are important factors in what one finds sexually attractive, and although the age-old Nature/Nurture debate will never be fully resolved with respect to same-sex attractions, we can at least agree that environment has a profound impact on subsequent behavior.

One way environment may impact behavior is with respect to disinhibition to experiment with homosexuality. In other words, a person's environment may play a role in sending the message that engaging in homosexual behavior is "okay," by affirming aspects of lifestyle, attractions, or behaviors. In some of the research conducted so far on prevalence rates of homosexuality, we know, for instance, that there are higher prevalence rates for homosexuality in urban settings than either suburban or rural settings.[2] While we do not want to make too much of these studies, they seem to suggest that one would do well to consider the many ways in which environment facilitates or undermines life goals.

Environment impacts our behaviors in many ways. For example, an individual struggling to remain sexually pure without throwing out his stash of pornography is sabotaging his goals by keeping certain items in his environment. Scripture directs us to flee from temptation. "Fleeing" is, in a sense, an extreme form of environment management. Pornographic materials and/or living in an area of a city where homosexuality is celebrated may hinder a person's ability to attain their goals. In this way environment management is a common sense approach to identifying and removing those things in your immediate environment that make it difficult for you to have the freedom to obtain, or maintain, chastity.

Michael Lundy and George Rekers, two experts on human sexuality, note that "reinforcement of patterns of behavior and thinking arises from multiple sources. Family interactions, opportunity, established sexual patterns of behavior, social and environmental cues, and the opportunity for privacy and anonymity are only a few."[3] Consequently, environment is extremely important, particularly as you consider facilitating the goals you have set for enjoying your life. Before we look more specifically at what it means to manage your environment, we want to introduce you to a concept that underlies much of our approach. We are referring to what it means to *identify* and *remove constraints.*

Identifying and Removing Constraints

According to one model of mental health, the concerns people have can be explained either positively or negatively. If you are struggling with depression, you could begin by investigating the causes of depression. Is it the way you are thinking? Perhaps you have a negative view of yourself. Or is your depression a result of a thyroid condition or a reaction to medications you are already taking? In any case, this is a *positive* explanation of depression because it focuses on the causes of depression. But you could also give a *negative* explanation: What is it that keeps you from experiencing happiness, contentedness, or satisfaction (feelings that would be present if you were not depressed)? Perhaps the things that keep you from satisfaction have to do with your relationships with your family or co-workers. Maybe your experience of happiness is constrained by the demands placed on you in the workplace or the way your employer relates to you in front of your co-workers. A negative explanation is intended to provide you with useful language for talking about and addressing your concerns in practical ways. From this perspective you identify and remove the constraints that make it difficult for you to experience happiness or satisfaction in the case of depression.

Consider the person who experiences same-sex thoughts, behaviors, or attractions and is pursuing change through our approach. A *positive* explanation for why a person experiences same-sex attraction or behavior might focus on genetic or prenatal hormonal predispositions, early parent-child relationships, or childhood sexual abuse. The focus is on what "causes" a homosexual identity or pattern of behavior. This is an important question for many people, and perhaps you are struggling with wanting an answer to this question yourself. Unfortunately, it may also be very difficult to determine with certainty what "caused" you to experience same-sex attraction.

Wanting to find out how to help his son, Jesse's father, Paul, sought out pastoral counseling. He thought that knowing the cause of Jesse's struggling would help pinpoint a "cure" or solution. Paul seemed plagued by a number of questions and determined to find the answers. "Why did this happen to our family and our son? How do we make the attractions go away? Did we do something wrong as parents? Did he get hurt as a baby?" His preoccupation with the search for a *positive* explanation for his son's same-sex attractions prevented Jesse's father from helping Jesse cope with his attractions and attain his goal of sexual purity.

In contrast to this, a *negative* explanation is concerned with what keeps a person from achieving their goals or becoming the kind of person they are striving to become. Again, with the client who experiences same-sex thoughts, behaviors, or attractions, the focus is more on what keeps these clients from achieving their goals, whether they are working toward chastity and fidelity, celibacy, sexual identity management, environment planning, or decreased homosexual thoughts and behaviors. So you may do well to begin to shift your focus away from why you are drawn to homosexual behaviors (a *positive* explanation) toward what keeps you from being able to achieve and maintain chastity or achieve another related goal (a *negative* explanation).

Hanging out with friends at a local lesbian coffee house was not helping matters for Cheryl. As a Christian, Cheryl wanted to live her life according to biblical principles and she could not resolve the issue of her same-sex relationship in light of Scripture. Cheryl decided to end her relationship, but she still held on to items that symbolized her previous lifestyle, and she socialized at local lesbian establishments. As part of Cheryl's process toward living faithfully before God, Cheryl began to examine those things that kept her from achieving her goals (that is, a *negative* explanation).

The theory behind this approach was discussed by Douglas Breunlin in an article in the *Journal of Marital and Family Therapy*. This theoretical approach is referred to as a "theory of constraints." When applied to people who experience same-sex attraction and behavior, the assumption is that people would be able to achieve and maintain their goals in life if they were not *constrained* in some way from doing so. This is an appropriate approach to homosexuality and same-sex attraction because it does not focus on pathology or mental illness, and as previously stated, major mental health organizations do not consider homosexuality to be a mental illness.[4] In the theory of constraints, the emphasis is on what keeps a person from solving his or her problem. The benefit to such a shift in emphasis is the focus on your strengths and competencies. It is meant to be a more forward thinking, constructive approach to helping you navigate the course of your life.

In the previous chapter, we focused on identifying habits and patterns impacting sexual attraction and behavior. In this chapter, we want to move further in helping you understand the dynamics that keep you stuck in unwanted behaviors. Think of it this way: By examining patterns we are acting like street cops, surveying the land and keeping a watchful eye out for damaging elements. In the next chapter, we are promoted to detective. Now, mind you, we haven't replaced our street cop skills, but are adding to the repertoire. There are many ways you can assess for constraints. We summarize one approach[5] that is actually organized around several points but, for our purposes, we limit this to the following factors: patterns, values, gender, development, and parts.

Patterns

It was mentioned in the last chapter that there are four classes of patterns or sequences. The four classes are (1) the brief, here-and-now interactions, (2) the daily/weekly routines of a person, (3) the longer patterns that can be measured in months, and (4) the generational patterns. Patterns that may be of concern as you contend with same-sex behavior and attraction have to do with how you relate to others, including family and friends, your daily routine, the weekly and monthly patterns of relating to others (and yourself), and generational patterns that contribute to your experiences, including what was said and modeled for you in the areas of sexual behavior and education.

Remember the belittling boss and his employee from the previous chapter? The employee stuffed their feelings of inferiority and rejection resulting from daily interactions with an emotionally abusive boss. They utilized food, television, and sad songs from previous relationships to soothe their anxieties of the day. Over time, days turned to weeks and weeks turned to months. Feeling out of control instead, this individual turned to an "old friend" for comfort.

Values

The values focus inevitably comes into play because everyone holds beliefs and values about specific behaviors. These beliefs and values can come from any number of sources, including your cultural background, religious upbringing or current religious commitments. These beliefs and values inform your thinking about sexuality and sexual behavior. How does your race, ethnicity, and religion contribute to how you view same-sex attraction and behavior? Does everyone in your family share the same religious beliefs? What has your family learned about human sexuality from their ethnicity or religious faith?

As you begin to reflect on these questions, an important consideration is whether the beliefs and values about sex that were modeled for you are beliefs and values you still hold today. In other words, do you claim these values as your own? If so, what led to that experience, that is, how did you come to accept the beliefs and values of your culture or ethnicity, or religion or family background as your own? When did you experience a shift, for example, from, "This is what my parents taught me," to "This is what I believe"?

Cheryl, in our example above, was raised in a devout Christian home and grew up believing in the authority of Scripture. Throughout her teen years she knew the sexual attractions she was experiencing did not line up with her religious beliefs or values. After struggling for years to embrace her same-sex attractions and a lesbian lifestyle, Cheryl decided to focus more on a relationship with Christ and honor her values and beliefs. Although difficult at times, her thoughts, feelings, and behaviors became more congruent to her life goals.

Gender

When considering gender, what seems most relevant to our approach is what you consider it means to be a man or a woman. This distinction refers to your biological sex ("sex"), and it also refers to your personal and social standing as male or female ("gender").

A place to begin may be to reflect upon what you learned from your family growing up about what it means to be a man or a woman. What did you learn from your father and your mother about what it means to be a man? What did they communicate to you about what it means to be a woman? What was considered masculine or feminine in your home? How did you know? Sometimes these messages are obvious to children, and you may have no trouble with identifying these messages; other times these messages are communicated through subtle messages or as much through what is *not* said or done as what *is* said and done.

Development

Development is concerned with your family life cycle and how you developed in relation to others. Family life cycle refers to how your family has gone through numerous stages of development: leaving home as a young adult, joining as a couple through marriage, families with young children, families with adolescents, launching children, and families in later life.[6] Each stage of life is characterized by a variety of challenges and significant changes that take place and that enable a person to make the needed adjustments to the demands of that stage in life. The life cycle has also been recently expanded to reflect the demands of single adults, single-parent families, and families facing divorce and remarriage.

To reflect on how you are developing in relation to others, you can consider biological, individual, relational, familial, and social development. In light of the present topic, an important consideration is that you may be wrestling with forming or maintaining an identity, and identity formation can be influenced at each of these levels.

Derek was about to become a father for the first time. His anxiety was through the roof. He had not thought of surfing the Internet for same-sex porn for over a year, but now with everything going on, he found himself wanting a distraction to soothe his anxiety. Tossing and turning through the night, Derek became paralyzed by the barrage of uncertainties. Will I be like my father? How can I possibly be responsible for another life? What will happen to my relationship with my wife?

Parts

As was briefly mentioned in the previous chapter, the focus on "parts" comes out of the work of Richard Schwartz, who focused on the person's internal experience. He essentially looked at the person and how that person was made up of different internal parts. This is intuitively obvious when you think about a specific decision you made, such as going to see the dentist. There may be a part of you that does not want to visit the dentist because you have had a history of painful associations with dentistry. At the same time, a part of you knows that you should follow through on the appointment because it is important for prevention of concerns of a more serious nature. One part of you might function to protect you from immediate discomfort but, ultimately, you have to make a decision. Your "self" steps in and decides to keep the appointment, despite having conflict among various "parts."

So although there is a "self" that can take a lead on decision-making and is responsible for your behavior, there are also "parts" that get into conflicts and form alliances just as families become conflicted and family members align with one another. This may help you see yourself more accurately as a person who has mixed feelings, but who is ultimately responsible for the decisions you make each day.

Levels of Constraints

According to Breunlin and his colleagues, constraints may also be experienced by people at the different levels: *biology*, *person*, *relationship*, *family*, *community*, and *society*. The challenge to clinicians is to identify constraints with reference to both *factors* (such as gender, values, religion or culture, and patterns) and *level*. For example, an adolescent female can experience constraints at the *relational* level if extreme parts of her conflict with extreme parts of her parents. This happens if the "rebellious" part of her is activated in response to the "controlling" part of her father, which is activated in relation to the "under-responsible" part of his spouse. So, she is in conflict with her parents, and they are in conflict with one another. The adolescent can also experience constraints at the *personal* level of her own mind. When this happens, various parts of her (her internal family system) are extreme, and some parts are in conflict, collude, form triangles, and so on. Her "rebellious" part may be in conflict with her "adult" part, the part of her that wants to be more responsible and trustworthy.

These concepts will become clearer if we consider an example. Albert presented in therapy and requested help in differentiating among his sexual identity concerns. He admitted to a longstanding attraction to the opposite sex and stated that he had only been in one or two heterosexual relationships, but without engaging in intercourse. However, he had spent the previous year experimenting in homosexual relationships and also regarded himself as a member of the gay community in a nearby city. He reported having had "numerous" same-sex partners. But despite having had only limited heterosexual relationship experience, he was nevertheless interested in developing his feelings of opposite-sex attraction. According to Albert, he chose to leave the gay lifestyle because of his religious values, but he did admit to feelings of ambivalence.

Albert described his relationship with his mother as close. His father had left the family when he was very young. His mother had had several boyfriends during Albert's childhood, but none were what he would describe as a father figure. Albert identified himself as a Christian who wanted to quit the gay lifestyle and pursue a life he believed to be more pleasing to God. But in so doing he also reported struggling with same-sex attraction to peers, intrusive thoughts, and isolation from potential supports. He especially wanted to surround himself with Christians who would value him, despite his current struggles with same-sex attraction.

Albert was also contending with difficulties in gender identification, as evidenced by his questions about masculinity and male roles in society, and expressed concerns by relating his own religious and cultural beliefs to larger cultural and religious ideas. Albert had questions about God's purposes for human sexuality and the morality of same-sex behavior. Finally, Albert had conflicts that can best be understood through "parts" language. There were fearful, guilty, and ashamed "parts" of Albert, as well as ambivalence towards experimenting with same-sex behavior, identifying with the gay community, and then leaving the gay community altogether.

In addition to constraints that might be identified through the overarching concepts of gender, "parts," and so on, Albert was also experiencing constraints at multiple *levels*. These included the levels of relationship and community. He may also have been experiencing constraints at the biological level—not insofar as biology *determines* same-sex attraction—but where biological antecedents may have predisposed him to same-sex attraction, or made same-sex relationships more appealing under certain circumstances. Constraints in a relationship occurred whenever Albert attempted to develop intimate, non-sexual friendships with men. He struggled with a desire for intimacy, but as he grew close to others, he equated closeness with genital sexual behavior. Albert also experienced constraints within the community when he realized that some members of the conservative Christian group he joined were unwilling to support him in his struggle with same-sex issues. This led to reports of isolation from potential supports.

Breunlin presents a four-step process for identifying and removing constraints: (1) identify presenting concerns and attempted solutions, (2) ask "constraint questions," (3) identify the constraint, and (4) discuss how to remove them. This process is illustrated in Figure 5.1. To follow the four steps, you might begin by thinking about a particular concern, such as a desire for non-sexual but intimate relationships. Or, you might ask a constraint question: "What prevents me from experiencing non-eroticized closeness with others? What would happen if I became emotionally close to another person but did not engage in sexual acts?" Perhaps the process of answering these questions will help you identify the constraint. Maybe you replied to the first question by admitting that in all your relationships you entangle sex with intimacy, and that you tend to eroticize relationships. Perhaps to the second question you expressed fear of rejection were you to become close to another person without engaging in the sex acts.

So what are the constraints? They apparently revolve around fears—fear of intimacy and fear of rejection. A key approach is to next consider ways to remove constraints.

Let us return to the case study above and, as a first step, identify Albert's presenting problem and his attempts to address it. Albert wanted help sifting through his sexual identity issues and he thought it prudent to resist same-sex relationships in order to confront his problem. His attempts to seek solutions included moving out of his city apartment where he had lived the previous year and join a conservative Christian community. Albert remarked on having struggled with a desire to discard phone numbers and gifts he had received from gay friends, some of which instigated and intensified his homosexual feelings.

The second step was to inquire into constraints. Ask, for example, "What keeps me from forming close but non-sexual same-sex relationships?" and "What prevents me from throwing away telephone numbers or gifts that are homosexually stimulating?" Albert answered the first question by saying that he experienced multiple constraints, including lack of *experience* (by having never known intimacy with another male that did not eventually involve sex), lack of *role modeling* (not seeing men in his family develop intimacy with one another), and lack of *opportunity* (finding that some members of the Christian community find it difficult to be close to someone struggling with same-sex attraction). Albert answered the second question by saying that he struggled at times with the sense of disconnection and loss that he might feel if he were to get rid of certain items. Some items were symbols of connection.

The third step was to discuss the constraints that become more apparent from the answers given to the constraint questions. For example, although Albert readily admitted that he wanted to get rid of the phone numbers and gifts, it became apparent that he had mixed feelings about them.

This brings up the fourth step: collaborating with Albert to remove constraints. This might take the form of discussing the "parts" that are in conflict in Albert. One part wants less exposure to same-sex stimulation. Another part wants to keep the items because that part was drawn to and missed same-sex relationships. Yet another part does not necessarily want to pursue same-sex relationships, but it longs for the sense of intimacy and connection that had been associated with sexual encounters, homosexual or heterosexual. Presumably, a protective part of Albert is afraid to risk additional changes, or to risk the experience of finality that might come with getting rid of these items. In some ways this is the heart of therapy, and it is a process. Over time Albert worked hard to sort through his ambivalent feelings and eventually chose to remove items in his environment to support his efforts at change. A summary of Albert's experience with the four-step process is illustrated in Figure 5.2.

We have already begun to address environment planning. Albert demonstrated his interest in managing his environment, and he was honest about his struggles in this area. So we turn now to what it means to intentionally reflect upon your environment and those things that facilitate or constrain your personal goals.

Environment Planning

According to Lundy and Rekers, "Environmental planning encompasses those strategies that an individual can use to change his or her environment, which, in turn, will exert a definite influence on behavior."[7] The place to begin is to identify the experiences, relationships, items, and so on that are in one's environment and facilitate same-sex thoughts, attraction, or behavior. These will vary from person to person. Let's take a look at three examples:

Sarah owns several items that are homosexually stimulating to her. These items are a shirt, pin, tie, picture, and candle. Some of the items were given as gifts, and others simply represent a time when she was actively involved in a close, intimate friendship that eventually developed into a sexual relationship.

In contrast to Sarah, John has fewer *items* of concern, but he struggles with places that represent to him something that sparks homosexual fantasies or a desire to act out through same-sex behavior or masturbation. These places include bars, playgrounds, bike paths, and rest rooms that John associates for whatever reason with same-sex behavior or fantasies.

Mary finds that certain relationships are particularly difficult for her in light of her treatment goals. Some of these relationships are past sex partners, while others are current friends with whom she experiences an emotional longing for connection.

Environment planning will vary for each person in each of these situations. For most people, environment planning will mean addressing concerns across all three areas: items, places, and relationships, but for the purposes of clarity we are separating them. For Sarah, environment planning may entail identifying and removing those items that are homosexually stimulating. She would probably admit that hanging onto those items is somewhat symbolic. Yet, this is Sarah's decision, and we should not underestimate her attachment to these symbols. And Sarah should work through her mixed feelings about these items before considering getting rid of them. So Sarah may want to consider whether there are "parts" of her that want certain items, while there are other "parts" that want her to make the decision to be rid of them. It may be that when Sarah is ready to get rid of the items, she will work through some of the grief and loss that giving them away represents.

For John, environment planning may include identifying the places that are homosexually stimulating and making a plan for not being in those places, including alternate routes to school or work, going shopping with a supportive friend, and so on. It may be important, then, that John have honest friendships where there is a sense of accountability around environment planning. This requires a friend or family member who knows about John's struggles and who is invited into a place of vulnerability so that the friend is able to speak freely out of love and respect for John.

Environment planning for Mary may entail working out plans in advance so that she is not alone with people to whom she is sexually attracted or with whom she is longing for a connection in a way that is inconsistent with her life goals. This can be difficult, and as with Sarah and John above, we would not want Mary to do anything rash to cut herself off from familiar and needed support systems. Any decision to do so should be done intentionally and deliberately after weighing the possible consequences.

A good place for you to begin is to look at Worksheet 5.1 and identify the items, places, and relationships that may be counterproductive to your personal goals. Then rate the degree to which you think that the item, place, or relationship is counterproductive. You could do this in the context of counseling or on your own, and you can use the worksheet at the outset of your work or anytime you wish to reflect intentionally on anything that you may feel has made it difficult for you to maintain your life goals. We encourage people to keep a journal, too, to reflect further on what they are seeing as they complete this worksheet.

For many people, as difficult as it is to get rid of items or to distance themselves from places that get in the way of their goals, the question of what to do with acquaintances and friendships is perhaps the most challenging. We do not want to underestimate this area of environment planning. The emphasis is not to sever relationships or meaningful support systems, because this can put you in a more vulnerable place than if you were to maintain some of those supports. But we would urge you to reflect on how to appropriately respond and relate when you have relationships with people who make working toward your goals more difficult.

A critical next step is to have you list the kinds of things you could do to manage your environment and to begin to think through the specific effects of making those changes. Use Worksheet 5.2 to help you think through some of the challenges you will face as you try to plan your environment.

For example, Robert realized that he struggled with the temptation to return to a gay bar he used to frequent. In his worksheet he wrote down, "Drive a different way home from work. Don't pass by the gay bar I used to visit." The practical impact for Robert was that he was "Less likely to stop or seek out a sexual partner." For Albert, specific gifts had become imbued with sexual meaning. He wrote down, "Remove gifts given to me by same-sex partners that may be sexually stimulating to me." Albert recognized that he would be "Less likely to be sexually stimulated by these gifts."

What is it about a specific item, place, or relationship that makes it so difficult to let go? Items and places especially can be symbols for something you feel or experience. How have these things become symbolic for you? Can you begin to unpack for yourself what these symbols mean? As you unpack the meaning of these items and places, can you begin to consider other ways to have those needs met in your life? This kind of shift could take weeks or months, and we do not want to underestimate this process in your life.

As you begin to have your needs met through other ways, you will also see how you are essentially re-symbolizing your life. What do we mean by this? As you begin to get your needs met through other means, these means become symbols of your new life goals. Take for example the concept of intimacy. Intimacy is symbolized differently for each person. Kate loved candles, and to Kate the burning of candles symbolized physical intimacy. Over time and many candles later, Kate's representation of intimacy was shifted or re-symbolized. Conversations with her accountability partner began to symbolize intimacy for Kate.

We have been focusing more on items and places, but let's consider relationships. Again, the same principles apply. If you are considering distancing yourself from acquaintances or friendships that you believe undermine your life goals, you will not want to simply live detached from meaningful relationships. Obviously, it would be ideal if existing friendships could support your attempts to realign your life around your beliefs and values. But if there are those who demean your decisions and your values, you may need to pursue other friendships that are much more supportive of your point of view.

What stands behind our understanding of environment planning is an understanding of constraints. Constraints are those things that keep us from achieving our goals, and as we have seen, they are critical to our understanding of environment planning. And, you will see that an accurate understanding of how to identify and remove constraints is an important concept for much of our approach.

Reflections on Environment Planning:

1. Take some time to shift your thinking about your struggles with same-sex attraction and behavior away from a positive explanation of causes to a negative explanation, where you reflect on those things that keep you from experiencing specific goals, such as chastity. How does this shift in language and perception help you identify and remove constraints?
2. Because constraints can be organized in the categories of patterns, values, gender, development, and parts, begin to sort through your specific experiences in each of these five areas. What are some of the themes you can identify that are essentially constraints? If you have a trusted friend or counselor to discuss this with, reflect together on what it would mean to meet your needs through other ways and remove existing constraints.

3. As you continue to reflect on constraints, what are some of the levels of constraints you experience? They might be at any or all of the following levels: *biology*, *person*, *relationship*, *family*, *community*, and *society*. Consider organizing your experiences of constraints around these six major categories so that you can begin to think of practical strategies for removing those constraints.
4. As you develop a rich and intricate account of constraints and begin to fulfill needs through behaviors consistent with your goals in life, you are essentially facilitating environment planning. There may also be several other concrete and practical things you can do to plan for and manage your environment, including identifying key items, places, and relationships that make meeting your life goals especially challenging.

Figure 5.1. Breunlin's Four-Step Process

Identify Presenting Concerns and Attempted Solutions

↓

Ask "Constraint Question"

↓

Identify the Constraint

↓

Discuss How to Remove the Constraints

Figure 5.2. Albert's Experience With the Four-Step Process

Identify Presenting Concerns and Attempted Solutions
- Wanted help sorting out sexual identity issues
- Wanted to stay out of same-sex relationships
- Desire to get rid of phone numbers and gifts that reminded him of same-sex attractions
- Attempted solutions: moving, becoming a part of Christian community

↓

Ask "Constraint Question"
- "What keeps you from forming close but non-sexual, same-sex relationships?"
- "What keeps you from getting rid of phone numbers or gifts that are homosexually stimulating to you?"

↓

Identify the Constraint
- Discuss constraints that became more apparent from the answers to questions
- Ex. "What keeps you from getting rid of phone numbers or gifts that are homosexually stimulating to you?" Answer: Mixed feelings about the phone numbers, what they represent, and so on.

↓

Discuss How to Remove the Constraints
- Collaborating with Albert to remove constraints
- Identifying patterns and habits
- Discussing "parts" that are in conflict
- Environment planning

Worksheet 5.1. Identifying Concerns in One's Environment

Identify and rate the concerns you have in the three following areas of environment management: items, places, and relationships:

Items	Places	Relationships
1. *rating* ___	1. *rating* ___	1. *rating* ___
2. *rating* ___	2. *rating* ___	2. *rating* ___
3. *rating* ___	3. *rating* ___	3. *rating* ___
4. *rating* ___	4. *rating* ___	4. *rating* ___

Rate the level of concern you have that this item, place, or relationship is counterproductive to your counseling goals:

0	1	2	3	4	5	6	7	8	9	10
None		Mild			Moderate		Significant		Very Significant	

Worksheet 5.2. Environment Management

Identify the changes you could make to your environment that would help you in light of treatment goals:

Specific Change to Environment	*Effect*
1. Drive home from work a different way so I don't pass by the gay bar I used to visit.	Less likely to stop there or seek out a sexual partner.
2. Remove gifts from same-sex partners that may be sexually stimulating.	Less likely to be sexually stimulated by these gifts.

Chapter

6

An Exchange: Old Scripts for New

Actors who play villainous roles sometimes report receiving hate mail. Actors are surprised, of course, because most actors are genuinely nice people; they make charitable contributions, and volunteer time to help others. Actors are essentially following a script that tells them how to identify and relate to others. If a particular actor plays a villain, follows the script written to elicit a particular reaction from the audience, and "sells" the audience on the believability of the character, some in the audience may confuse the actor with the character portrayed. In fact, sometimes actors intentionally seek out parts for television, theatre, or movies that reflect a sharp contrast to the character for which they are most known. If they read from another script—and if they capture the complexities of another character—they can combat their image as a villain.

We often refer to "scripts" when we help people who contend with same-sex attraction and behavior. Because actors are given a script, they are essentially portraying a character based on the skills and qualities they have within themselves. Of course, scripts are written, edited, and rewritten time and time again, so there is great flexibility when one thinks of one's life as something like reading from a script. You can question where you got the script from which you have been reading. You can do more than question the origins of the script—who wrote it, who expects you to read from it perfectly, and so on—you can also edit the script you have been given. It is in that spirit that this chapter focuses on how you identify yourself to others in public and to yourself in private. The question of identity we will think about as a "script," which suggests something you read from—just like an actor.

When you think about scripts in relation to your experiences of same-sex attraction, think both about how you think of your experiences of same-sex attraction, as well as how you think of yourself with respect to your identity. Throwing herself on the sofa, Sally proclaimed, "I am gay. I can't get rid of these feelings, and I have tried everything. I am putting a pink triangle on my car and getting on with my life as a lesbian." Sally identified herself as a lesbian from her experiences with same-sex attractions. Unfortunately, she neglected to identify herself by the other dimensions of her identity: a daughter, a Christian, or a mother. Sally's scripts keep her frustrated and defeated by her experiences of same-sex attractions and centered on the belief that homosexual attractions are evidence of a gay identity.

From a sexual identity management perspective, this brings up two broad approaches to helping people who contend with same-sex attraction and seek change: chastity and reorientation. We think of these not as discrete categories that are inherently mutually exclusive, but as existing in relation to one another in such a way that there is some overlap.

The first approach is a *chastity-based* approach. Proponents of this approach tend to think that orientation may not change, but they firmly believe that people can choose how they live and how they present themselves to others. While orientation may or may not change, people can always take responsibility for their behavior. Chastity, then, is expressed in both thoughts and behaviors. From a Christian sexual ethic's perspective, chastity in relationships is a goal to which all Christians should aspire.

A variation on the chastity-based approach is *freedom from homosexuality*. This approach is characterized by helping people get out of the gay lifestyle and to not act compulsively on same-sex attractions. The person may or may not experience a change of orientation—again, it is not the focus—but they do experience freedom from homosexual thoughts and behaviors that had consumed a lot of their time and energy.

Taking a different approach to sexual identity management, *reorientation approaches* focus intentionally and specifically on changing a person's sexual orientation from homosexual to heterosexual. Proponents of this view might look at a chastity-based approach as an option, but embrace reorientation as a more desirable goal. We would like to help you feel some freedom in drawing upon elements from each of these perspectives without fully committing yourself to any one. Our process principally draws upon chastity-based and freedom from homosexuality approaches that leaves one open to experiencing change, while drawing upon principles that may facilitate that process and may help you coordinate sexual identity management. So our approach is rather broad and multifaceted.

Sexual Identity and Attributions

We began this chapter by noting that scripts can be understood with respect to why a person experiences same-sex attraction, and we mentioned that scripts can also reflect the context within which a person makes meaning of their current experiences of same-sex attraction. What do we mean by this? If at one time you had adopted a gay identity, or if you are struggling with this now, ask yourself who wrote the script you read telling you that your experiences of same-sex attraction mean that you are gay? If you are like others, you might say that the broader culture has helped to write this script. Or perhaps the media and the entertainment industry has penned a few words, as much has been communicated about normative experiences for establishing a "gay" identity. Maybe members of the "gay" community have been telling you to be honest with yourself about your gay identity. Sometimes people say to us that they "always knew" that their experiences of same-sex attraction meant that they were gay. However, since the self-defining attribution has only been made in Western culture at this time in history, there are probably other factors influencing this belief, even if it seems to have been longstanding. If you have long believed yourself to be gay, where did your beliefs come from? You may have "always known" you were different, but you had to at some point attribute feeling different to something, and you may have organized your beliefs and perceptions around your experiences of same-sex attraction, thereby taking on a gay identity as a reflection of the culture within which you were raised.

The questions we want you to keep in mind as we continue to unpack what it means to have a sexual identity include: Who wrote the script you have been reading from? Can it be rewritten? Can it be edited? Can you work with others to write a new chapter?

If you are like most people who struggle in this area and are pursuing alternatives, multiple sources have shaped and reinforced how you think about your experiences of same-sex attraction. For the most part these sources have one thing in common: they presume that same-sex attraction means that you should take on a "gay" identity. This is the culture and time we live in. It may be beneficial for you to reflect on the cultural climate. Herdt, a gay theorist, identified four forms of homosexuality across cultures: (1) *age-structured homosexuality* (for example, initiation ceremonies in some societies in New Guinea); (2) *gender-reversed homosexuality* (for example, North American Indian *berdache*); (3) *role-specialized homosexuality* (for example, the Chukchee shaman whose vision quest directs him to engage in same-sex behavior for a time); and (4) *the modern gay movement*. According to Herdt, the modern gay movement is qualitatively different from other forms of homosexuality, and "only by disengaging sexuality from the traditions of family, reproduction, and parenthood was the evolution of the gay movement a social and historical likelihood."[1] One dimension to the modern gay movement that is a significant departure from any other expression of homosexuality in other cultures and throughout other ages, is the self-defining attribution: "I am gay."

At one level, people are not "gay" or "straight." These are labels we use to say something about a person's experiences of same- or opposite-sex attractions. In our approach, we utilize descriptive language that reflects, shapes, and reshapes your identity and experience. You experience same-sex attraction, and so we use this language to reflect your experience. The language, in turn, shapes your identity, as you begin to see yourself as a person who experiences same-sex attraction in different settings or in different relationships. This language also reshapes your identity and experience by allowing you to accurately describe your experiences (so you avoid denial or minimization), while empowering you to identify with other parts of who you are as a person.

Before we turn to other aspects of who you are as a person, let us not neglect to say something further about your experiences of sexual attraction. Worksheet 6.1 shows a scale from 1–10 where "1" represents no opposite-sex attraction, and "10" represents significant opposite-sex attraction. What number would you give yourself today? Keep that in mind as you consider another scale, also numbered from 1–10. On this second scale "1" represents no same-sex attraction, and "10" represents significant same-sex attraction, what number would you give yourself today? This worksheet can be used at the outset and once every month or every few months to track how your experiences of same-sex attraction change over time.

In our experience many people who report same-sex attractions also report some opposite-sex attractions. If that is your experience, then that is a part of yourself you may choose to identify with as you work on sexual identity management. Accepting a script that says having homosexual attractions means you are gay ignores as meaningful any opposite sex attractions. Some individuals contend that the presence of homosexual attractions negates opposite attractions, thus labeling himself or herself as gay or lesbian.

How do you identify with the part of yourself that experiences opposite-sex attraction? The answer to this question will vary from person to person in part because some people may report a "5" or higher on opposite-sex attractions and a "5" or less on same-sex attractions, while others may report just the opposite. We offer a few principles for identifying with the part of you that experiences opposite-sex attraction. These principles reflect and are consistent with the themes addressed throughout this book:

1. Pay attention to the ways in which your daily patterns or routines may facilitate opposite- and same-sex attraction.
2. Identify key items, places, and relationships that may fuel same-sex attractions and locate symbolic items, places, and cultivate relationships that reflect your beliefs and values as they pertain to chastity or reinforce your existing opposite-sex attractions.
3. Avoid denying or minimizing your experiences of same-sex attraction. Go back to the rating you gave yourself and be honest in saying, "Yes, I experience same-sex attractions, but they do not define who I am as a person." Do not feel obligated to tell yourself or anybody else that same-sex feelings have diminished if they have not. In fact, they may ebb and flow for a time in ways that reflect other things that are going on in your life.
4. Avoid amplifying in your own mind your experiences of same-sex attraction. When people see value in not denying their experiences of same-sex attraction, they sometimes struggle with finding a balance. They may amplify their experiences by ways in which they cope or fail to cope and may overreact to their attractions.

How do sexual identity and attributions relate to replacing old scripts with new? Let us return to the rating you gave yourself earlier in the chapter. Even if you report a score of "1" on opposite-sex attraction and a score of "10" on same-sex attraction, you can still make choices about sexual identity management. And if you experience a change in how you would rate yourself on these scales in the future, you can always revisit sexual identity management in light of increased opposite-sex attractions and decreased same-sex attractions if that should be your experience.

How is it *empowering* to identify with your position in Christ, or your gender, or your ethnicity, or any other aspect of who you are as a person? To empower means to give or share power with, and we believe you are reclaiming your identity by intentionally determining which aspects of yourself you identify with. You can choose to identify with your experiences of same-sex attraction. Many people do this. At this time in our culture's history, we describe these people as "gay" or "lesbian." They describe themselves in the same way. They self-identify as "gay" or "lesbian." They make a self-defining attribution. They attribute their same-sex attractions as more central to their identity, and they integrate their experiences of same-sex attraction into a gay or lesbian identity. You could do this. But our approach also empowers you to choose alternatives to integrating your attractions into a gay or lesbian identity. You can dis-identify with these attractions, which means you are honest about experiencing them while intentionally choosing to see them as at the periphery of who you are as a person. In other words, you do not believe that they define who you are as a person. They are redefined and old scripts are replaced with new scripts. These experiences of same-sex attraction are one part of who you are as a whole person. By dis-identifying with these attractions, you are free to identify with other parts of who you are. What are these other parts of who you are? It depends. If you are religiously-affiliated, your identity may include a religious identity, for example, you may have an identity as a Christian, Jew, Muslim, or Mormon. Because you are male or female, you might identify with your gender as more central to who you are as a person. If you are married or if you have children, you might identify more with your standing as a husband or wife, or father or mother. And there are several other dimensions to your identity, such as your ethnicity, race, and so on.

Sexual Identity Management

Sexual identity management refers to the intentional practice of determining which aspect of yourself you choose to identify with and how you then present yourself to others. In order to facilitate sexual identity management, you may benefit from a few practical strategies: an imagery exercise, reflection on self-identification, and self-identification in public/private.

Imagery Exercise

Consider the following imagery exercise as one approach to helping you recognize other aspects of who you are as a person:

> *Close your eyes and breathe deeply, exhaling slowly. Repeat this three times… Now imagine yourself—who you are as a person—as a blank screen. You might imagine this as a television*

screen or a computer screen. Imagine that this blank screen is divided in half vertically, right down the middle. On the left side of the screen are your experiences of same-sex behavior. All of your experiences of same-sex behavior are on the left side of the screen. Now take a look at what is on the right side of the screen. What do you see?

A variation on this is to do the imagery exercise and place same-sex attractions, thoughts, or fantasies on the left side of the screen. The only caution we would share around using same-sex attraction or sexual orientation is that we do not think it is best to work to distance yourself from your experiences of same-sex attraction if distancing yourself would seem to deny or minimize the fact that you have these attractions. It seems to work best to acknowledge that these attractions exist and consider how they may be made smaller and less influential, as well as ways in which they may signal some kind of unmet need, as some theories suggest, rather than to deny, minimize, or reject them out of hand.

One woman shared how she had been in counseling for some time but had not experienced a change of sexual orientation; however, she felt as though her experiences of same-sex attraction were "smaller" and more manageable. She likened them to an icon on a computer screen: Using the coping skills she had learned, she was able to minimize the icon, whereas prior to her efforts her experiences of same-sex attraction were maximized on the screen, that is, they took up the whole screen and were unmanageable.

In a sense we are talking about integrating experiences of same-sex attraction into who you are as a particular person rather than either cutting them off from who you are or seeing them as central to (or at the core of) who you are as a particular person.

Self-Identification

Another exercise is to rate the top three or more ways in which you identify yourself in private and in public. Use Worksheet 6.2 to rank order the many ways you identify yourself in private. If you were to ask, "What kind of person am I?" what would you answer? Use your journal to reflect upon your rankings and what they say about your identity and how you think about yourself.

Then rank the top three or so preferred ways you identify to your own family, friends, and co-workers. Again, journal your reactions to what you have ranked. What do your rankings mean to you? As you reflect on what you have written, you have information that may help you more clearly see how you identify yourself in private and in public.

Sexual Identity Management

The third exercise is to identify your current primary and secondary identity (for example, gay, lesbian, bisexual, heterosexual, ex-gay, ex-ex-gay, religious, etc.) and then your ideal primary and secondary identity. Look at Worksheet 6.3 and reflect upon how you actually identify yourself to others and how you would like to identify yourself to others if you could have your ideal.

Also, reflect upon how you currently identify yourself to your family, friends, and co-workers, as well as how you would ideally like to identify yourself to your family, friends, and co-workers. Continue to add your thoughts to your journal.

The emphasis in this exercise on your current and ideal ways of identifying to yourself and to others is important as it helps you learn that you can hold out a vision for the kind of person you want to be, or at least the ways in which you might identify to yourself in private and to others in public.

Both approaches to this exercise are intended to remind you that there are many aspects to your identity, and that same-sex attraction is merely one such aspect. Of course, a person's sexual attraction is an important aspect of identity to oneself and to others. However, it is not the only or even most central aspect of identity, and this realization alone can aid in expanding the alternatives you experience to same-sex attraction and behavior.

The essential issue is that you can choose to integrate your experiences of same-sex attraction into a gay, lesbian, or bisexual identity, or you can live with experiences of same-sex attraction but not have those experiences define your identity. The issues addressed so far in this chapter should also be understood in the broader context of a practical theology of sanctification (more on that in Chapter 7).

Scripts and Meaning-Making

Let us return to construing scripts as germane to how you think about your experiences of same-sex attraction. A study presented recently at the American Psychiatric Association reported that there was a relationship between self-reported changes in sexual attraction (decreased same-sex attraction and self-reported changes of orientation) and how a person thought about the meaning of their same-sex attractions. Although many people in the "gay" community presume that experiences of same-sex attraction mean only one thing, that is, that you are a gay, lesbian, or bisexual person, these reports of successful change told a different story. They reported that one thing that helped them on the road to change was to think of their sexual attractions as meaningful, but not as defining who they are as a person. The meanings may vary from person to person, but one prominent theme seen in this literature is that these same-sex attractions were suggestive of a longing for connection with a parent, most often the parent of the same-sex who may have been critical, distant, or absent. Intervention, then, often focuses on meeting unmet emotional needs with members of the same sex. Although the research is mixed[2] as to whether there is support for this theory, it has come up again and again in the literature, and it may be worth exploring further, especially if a script that accounts for same-sex attraction may be related to experiences of successful change.

Another study[3] reported that just having an alternative framework for interpreting the meaning of same-sex attractions was enough to lead to changes in self-reported experiences of same-sex attraction and orientation. In other words they did not get very far in meeting these unmet same-sex needs; they attributed change to meaning making, to having gained insight into another way of thinking about what their same-sex attractions may mean.

We will mention just one other study[4] of women who dis-identified with their experiences of same-sex attraction. For these "ex-lesbians," again change appeared to be related to an alternate construal for meaning making. They construed the meaning behind their same-sex attraction differently, and their reinterpretation of their "story" or "script," coupled with the social support they received in a religion-based support group, facilitated a change in their self-reported sexual identity.

Parent-Child Relationships

We mentioned earlier that one of the most frequently discussed stories or scripts having to do with same-sex attraction implicates early childhood relationships, particularly parent-children relationships. Of those theories that implicate parent-child relationships in the origins of same-sex attraction and homosexual orientation, psychoanalytic theory has by far been the most prominent. In this theory, what is believed to cause male homosexuality is a combination of a close-binding mother and a rejecting or emotionally detached father. Essentially, males are heterosexual to the extent that they develop a secure male identity. If this does not happen—if a young male experiences his father as emotionally absent or unavailable and his mother as emotionally overwhelming or highly critical of males—then he may develop a sexualized longing for male closeness.

It should be noted that this theory may not apply to everyone who experiences same-sex attraction. If you reflect on your own family upbringing and your experiences of same-sex attraction and find that your parent-child relationship is consistent with this theory, it may be helpful to you to consider whether or not the desire to be emotionally close to members of the same-sex is a normal developmental need that may have gone unmet. If so, present desires to connect with members of the same sex may be experienced as compelling and may become sexually charged. These may be essentially misidentified by your sense of sexual desire as intimacy and emotional closeness when it is acted on physically through genital sexual expression.

For those who find that this theory seems to fit their experience, three levels of interest in connecting with those of the same-sex may be evident. These are (1) a desire to connect emotionally with some members of the same sex, (2) a fascination with some members of the same sex, to be validated by them, and it may include a sense of being compelled to be close to them, and (3) a sexually charged fascination with members of the same sex.

Some people who experience same-sex attraction are quite clear that they see a connection between their present experiences of same-sex attraction and their longing to meet emotional needs that were unmet by their same-sex parent. Consider the following case example.

Brett presented in therapy with concerns about his experiences of same-sex attraction and made connections between his present experiences of sexual attraction and his past experiences of emotional neglect. He had been reading about people who had experienced change of sexual behavior and orientation, and he wanted to work toward such a change. After explaining the research in this area and working through advanced informed consent to therapy, Brett shared what he felt was a particularly important dimension to his experiences of sexual attraction. He described his father as unemotional and uninvolved with his family. Though physically present, he was emotionally absent. Brett described his mother as emotionally close, and he expressed some concern that he may be too emotionally dependent upon her. As we discussed past experiences of same-sex attraction, Brett shared a particularly painful experience of rejection by a past employer, who he felt particularly drawn to emotionally. In fact, Brett referred to this attraction as "being compelled" to be connected with him emotionally and having an "emotional fascination" with him. He began to share his own emerging conclusion that what became a sexually charged emotional fascination with this man was related to his own sense of loss for not having had an emotionally satisfying relationship with his father. Brett was able to replace 'old scripts' for new and could define his sexual attractions and experiences in a more comprehensive manner.

You can begin to think through your experiences in this area by describing your relationship with your father and mother. You might reflect on this both before age 15 and at present. The years before age 15 represent your childhood experience of emotional connection and sense of boundaries with each parent. You can essentially reflect on your sense of closeness, emotional connection, intimacy, emotional boundaries, and affection in relation to both your father (Worksheet 6.4) and mother (Worksheet 6.5). Take some time to reflect on and journal about your relationship with your father and mother, especially with respect to closeness and affection.

You might also benefit from thinking about the messages you heard when you learned about what it means to be a man or a woman. These messages come from any number of sources, but they are often learned through interactions with your parents. Use Worksheet 6.6 to identify the messages you heard (or did not hear) from both of your parents, as well as others. You might then reflect on what stands out from what you are writing. This provides a good opportunity to discuss what it means to be a man or a woman, how these messages are communicated, and how culture, including the media, the entertainment industry, and other sources, can impact our views.

You can also consider a non-family member of the same sex (for example, a college roommate, co-worker, employer, and so on) with whom you have noticed a desire to feel a greater sense of emotional connection or closeness. Using Worksheet 6.7, think about the extent to which you would like to *connect emotionally* with that person. Also consider the degree to which you feel *fascinated* (or *compelled* to connect) with this person. Then reflect on the extent to which you experience a *sexually charged fascination* with this person. You can then reflect on your responses to these questions and consider where you may be seeking to meet unmet emotional needs through sexual behavior.

Of course, if this theory seems to fit your experiences, you may want to then identify how you can meet your emotional needs in ways consistent with your goals in life. One such approach would be to develop emotionally meaningful relationships with members of the same sex where there is little risk of sexually acting out behavior. Consistent with this theory, this can begin through the course of therapy if the therapist and client are of the same gender, and the questions and conflicts surrounding emotional intensity can be processed in a safe and therapeutic relationship. You could then work with your therapist to generalize your success in the therapy relationship to other relationships outside of therapy. This is sometimes when therapists consider a referral to a support group, but it is also possible to pursue emotionally meaningful relationships outside of therapy with one or two people who present little risk of sexually acting out behavior.

A Word to Sexual Abuse Survivors

Before we close this chapter we want to reflect on some of the identity and related issues faced by sexual abuse survivors. We want to reiterate that not everyone who experiences same-sex attraction reports a history of sexual abuse; and the experience of sexual abuse does not directly cause homosexuality, though it may be one among several factors that may make same-sex attraction a possibility for some people.

Our Choice of Words

Mike Lew, in his book *Victims No Longer*,[5] offers a helpful distinction between thinking of yourself as a *victim* of abuse and thinking of yourself as a *survivor* of abuse. According to Lew, the word "victim" accurately conveys what is true about sexual abuse, because the child experiences abuse through no fault of his or her own. But the word itself also connotes helplessness, and so it may only be an accurate word to use when you think about your experience or condition during the time you were abused.

The word "survivor," in contrast, says something very different about you. It means you have endured a very difficult hardship. Lew points out that one image that comes to mind is that of a person "clinging to flotsam while their ship sinks."[6] So the image is that of the survivors of the Titanic or some other shipwreck hanging on until someone comes to rescue them. Those who survived endured the hardship, and this kind of endurance is an important survivor quality to identify with; however, being able to endure hardship points to the inherent limitations of the word itself, because it is "a temporary state, one that will be replaced by something better."[7] That "something better" may be experiencing a more satisfying life, experiencing an increased quality of life, or learning to thrive and delight in relationships with oneself and others.

Moving from Victim to Survivor

What does it look like to move from victim to survivor? How do you know when you have arrived or embraced a survivor's mentality? Women in circles of our society are still thought of as the weaker sex. The perspective of a woman as helpless and powerless sets a victim tone for many. Overcoming the devastating consequences of sexual abuse seems unattainable for some. Trapped in a world filled with memories and emotions of the abuse, some resign themselves to "getting by" each day. Numbed by the abusive acts of others and their debilitating reactions to the abuse, these individuals have long forgotten what it feels like to be alive. Without the help of God and others, and the volition to make changes in their thoughts, feelings, and behaviors, victims of sexual abuse will remain in a destructive cycle, opting to remain a casualty of the insidious darkness shrouding this form of abuse.

Individuals struggling with the aftermath of sexual abuse often find it difficult to talk about the abuse and the lasting consequences they face. Their thoughts and feelings about themselves, and their abuser(s) are kept churning inside as they attempt to find the means to cope with the painful memories. Sexual abuse has tarnished their view of themselves as children of God and of God as their father. One reason that it is difficult for individuals to talk about their sexual abuse is that the subject matter is still somewhat of a taboo, especially in church communities. Well-meaning people, unsure of how to respond, are more likely to offer Scriptures and "get over it" prayers to the wounds of a survivor.

Individuals who have experienced sexual abuse are more likely to "get stuck" in their recovery due to issues related to safety and trust. Isolation is all too prevalent among victims of sexual abuse. But isolation to some is equivalent to safety. Avoiding relationships and social engagements provides a protective barrier for some; however, the lasting consequences of this separation keep the individual from what he/she needs most—a restorative community, a place where victims are embraced, encouraged to face the abuse, and empowered to make healing choices.

One of the complications for men is that it is socially *un*acceptable to see men as victims. Men are socialized to be protectors of themselves and of others, and so it is difficult for our society to know how to respond to men who were victimized as children. And men struggle with how to respond to their abuse. As Lew observes, men often feel emasculated by the experience, and some may attempt to prove their masculinity through risk-taking behaviors, while others may give up on moving forward or may feel pressure to hide the abuse from others.

Rollo struggled with his identity as a survivor of sexual abuse. He had been sexually abused by an extended family member when he was a boy, and the experience left him with real questions about his identity as a male, and these were particularly difficult for him as he became a young adult. It was not until he was well into his thirties that he felt he could face his experiences in the context of counseling. He often thought of himself and spoke of himself as a victim of sexual abuse, and it took several months for him to begin to feel like a survivor of the abuse he had experienced.

For both men and women alike, it is important to think and talk about yourself using words that convey your status as a survivor rather than a victim. This includes making "I" statements: being able to say, "I will get involved with this activity," as opposed to passively waiting for others to make it happen.

Self-care is important for maintaining a survivor rather than a victim identity. This means being able to ask yourself questions like, "What are the things that I need today?" For Christians this is set in a context: "What are the things that God is telling me I need today?" Those who are moving from victim to survivor have increased success asking themselves these kinds of questions and taking responsibility to find the answers to such questions.

Maintaining good boundaries with others is important. This involves knowing where you begin and end in terms of your emotional state and how you relate and react to the concerns and expectations of others. Rollo often related to his wife out of a victim posture. He struggled with his tendency to overreact in arguments with his wife. He was easily defensive and spoke out of past emotional and sexual injuries that she had nothing to do with. Over time, he made improvements. He began to stop himself at the early stages of angry, defensive reactions to his wife, and he began to see that his reactions, while indicative of protective survival skills in childhood, were now getting in the way of his ability to enjoy intimacy with his partner.

Are there times when you react out of a victim posture? Can you identify the face-to-face exchanges, daily patterns, or weekly routines that complicate this for you? Eliana Gil writes about "decoding and supporting the intent of the symptom."[8] This refers to being able to understand when your behavior is related to the effects of abuse, as when you feel small and helpless in relation to a co-worker and find yourself acting out in self-destructive ways because you have not worked through a passive style of relating to others. It is extremely important for survivors to grieve their losses and their pain. Confronting and addressing the memories of traumatic experiences can be challenging and at times downright scary. So often survivors are encouraged to "get over it" or "let it go." To move to a place of restoration, one cannot go around a place of mourning. We are not advocating that you remain stuck in the past, but it is important to deal with past abuse.

Are there times when you attempt to push away or deny the pain of the past? How is holding in or holding on to the pain of yesterday impacting the choices you make about yourself and others? What routines or patterns have you developed to help you avoid looking at painful memories? As you grieve the losses of yesterday, we encourage you to maintain a "kingdom attitude" for tomorrow. What we mean by this is that as you walk through a place of restoration, hold fast to the future. You may need the help of a friend or a counselor to come alongside you through this process.

Never underestimate the power of change. Change may be exciting for you; it may also be unsettling. This is important to remember as you make changes in your thoughts, feelings, and behaviors. As you begin to identify and make changes in your face-to-face exchanges, daily patterns, and weekly routines, the world, your friends, family, and yourself may seem different. Someone said once that courage was action in the presence of fear. Change often brings the unknown, a state of a myriad of possibilities. With these possibilities come choices, whether it be choices of freedom and life or choices leading to stagnation and unhealthy ways of relating. Are there times when you choose to relate as a victim, when change catches you off guard and you return to unhealthy ways of relating? Can you identify ways in which you structure your daily activities and weekly routines to avoid that which may become unpredictable? In which areas of your life have you changed?

As you begin to make healthier choices for yourself, we encourage you to celebrate. Celebrate? Yes, celebrate those markers, whether they are in inches, feet, yards, or miles. Beverly Engel writes about this important aspect of the healing process and encourages survivors to care for themselves by celebrating success, big or small.[9] Whether you have the courage to set a boundary in a relationship or have just appropriately expressed disappointment with a friend, consolidate your gains and celebrate.

Sarah, a survivor of sexual abuse, initially had some difficulties celebrating gains in treatment. She thought celebrating was a prideful act that took her focus off of Christ, as the author and finisher of her faith. Over the course of the next couple of months, Sarah began to embrace God as being on "her team," as one who was cheering her on as she surrendered to His work of restoration in her life. This may be a helpful way to pray, asking God to help you see more clearly and more accurately who He is in the midst of your experiences, what it means at a practical level to experience God as on your side.

Reflections on Identity:

1. What is your current rating of opposite-sex attraction, and what is your current rating of same-sex attraction? Have these ratings changed over the years? Might the ratings even fluctuate somewhat from week to week, or month to month? If so, what do you think contributes to those fluctuations? Begin to track patterns and routines with an eye for the impact they have on your attractions and consider routines and relationships that are commensurate with your life goals.
2. Setting aside the question of sexual attractions, what are other aspects of you as a person with which you feel you can identify? How do you see yourself with respect to religion? What do you identify with in terms of your sex? How about your status as a husband or a wife? What about your ethnicity or race?
3. Would you say that your experiences growing up reflect the theory discussed about parent-child relationships? If so, what do you think of the theory? How would things be different if you began to think of your experiences of same-sex attraction as reflecting a healthy, normal longing for connection and identification with a significant same-sex figure, such as a parent?
4. Have you experienced a desire to connect emotionally with some members of the same sex? Have you felt a fascination for some members of the same sex—a desire to be validated by them, or feeling as if you were compelled to be close to them? Have you ever experienced a sexually charged fascination with someone of the same sex? As you reflect on your answers to these questions, how do you make sense of your answers? What attributions do you make? How do your attribu-

tions reflect your beliefs and assumptions about your sexual identity? Are there other attributions you might make that would be consistent with your life goals?

5. If you experienced sexual abuse in your past would you identify yourself today as a victim of abuse or a survivor of abuse? Can you say that you are beyond mere survival? What word would you use to convey your experience—thriving? What other words come to mind? If you are working through the process of moving from victim to survivor, what steps can you take to move in that direction? Identify concrete and practical gains that you have made to date. What things can you do today to continue on the path of healing?

Worksheet 6.1. Sexual Attraction Thermometer

Directions: Please circle the number that best represents your current level of sexual attraction:

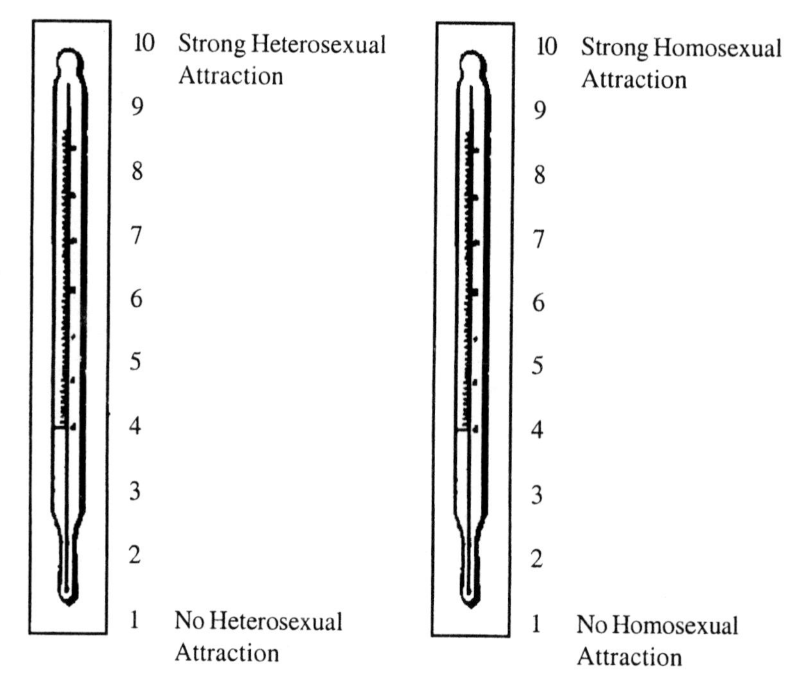

Worksheet 6.2. Sexual Identity Management—Private/Public

Please identify your CURRENT top 2–3 aspects of your identity as you think privately of yourself. Also note your ideal private identification.

- ☐ Gay/Lesbian/Bisexual
- ☐ Heterosexual/straight
- ☐ Ex-gay
- ☐ Ex-ex-gay
- ☐ Religious (e.g., Christian, Jew, Muslim)
- ☐ Gender (e.g., male, female)
- ☐ Other (please specify): ______________________

What do these identities mean to you?

Current:

____

____

____

Ideal:

____

____

____

Please identify your CURRENT top 2–3 aspects of your identity as you present yourself to others. Also note your ideal public identification.

- ☐ Gay/Lesbian/Bisexual
- ☐ Heterosexual/straight
- ☐ Ex-gay
- ☐ Ex-ex-gay
- ☐ Religious (e.g., Christian, Jew, Muslim)
- ☐ Gender (e.g., male, female)
- ☐ Other (please specify): ______________________

What do these identities mean to you?

Current:

____

____

____

Ideal:

____

____

____

Worksheet 6.3. Self-Identification

How do you identify yourself to yourself? Please write in your identification based on each of the categories below, then rank them (1–3), so that 1 = most important aspect of self-identity, 2 = next most important aspect of self-identity, and 3 = the next most important aspect of self-identity.

Current

- ☐ Race: "I am Black/White/Asian."
- ☐ Sex: "I am male/female."
- ☐ Sexual orientation: "I am homo-/heterosexual."
- ☐ Religious affiliation: "I am a Christian."
- ☐ Nationality: "I am an American."
- ☐ Ethnicity: "I am Puerto Rican."
- ☐ Other (please specify): "I am ______________."

Ideal

- ☐ Race: "I am Black/White/Asian."
- ☐ Sex: "I am male/female."
- ☐ Sexual orientation: "I am homo-/heterosexual."
- ☐ Religious affiliation: "I am a Christian."
- ☐ Nationality: "I am an American."
- ☐ Ethnicity: "I am Puerto Rican."
- ☐ Other (please specify): "I am ______________."

How do you identify yourself to others (family, friends, co-workers)? Please write in your identification based on each of the categories below, then rank them (1–3), so that 1 = most important aspect of self-identity, 2 = next most important aspect of self-identity, and 3 = the next most important aspect of self-identity.

Current

- ☐ Race: "I am Black/White/Asian."
- ☐ Sex: "I am male/female."
- ☐ Sexual orientation: "I am homo-/heterosexual."
- ☐ Religious affiliation: "I am a Christian."
- ☐ Nationality: "I am an American."
- ☐ Ethnicity: "I am Puerto Rican."
- ☐ Other (please specify): "I am ______________."

Ideal

- ☐ Race: "I am Black/White/Asian."
- ☐ Sex: "I am male/female."
- ☐ Sexual orientation: "I am homo-/heterosexual."
- ☐ Religious affiliation: "I am a Christian."
- ☐ Nationality: "I am an American."
- ☐ Ethnicity: "I am Puerto Rican."
- ☐ Other (please specify): "I am ______________."

Worksheet 6.4. Relationship with Father

1. Rate the degree of emotional closeness between you and your father before age 15:

0 1 2 3 4 5 6 7 8 9 10

Not Close Moderately Close Very Close

Describe your relationship with your father before age 15 (discuss sense of closeness, emotional connection, intimacy, emotional boundaries, affection):

____

____

____

____

2. Rate the degree of emotional closeness between you and your father today:

0 1 2 3 4 5 6 7 8 9 10

Not Close Moderately Close Very Close

Describe your relationship with your father today (discuss sense of closeness, emotional connection, intimacy, emotional boundaries, affection):

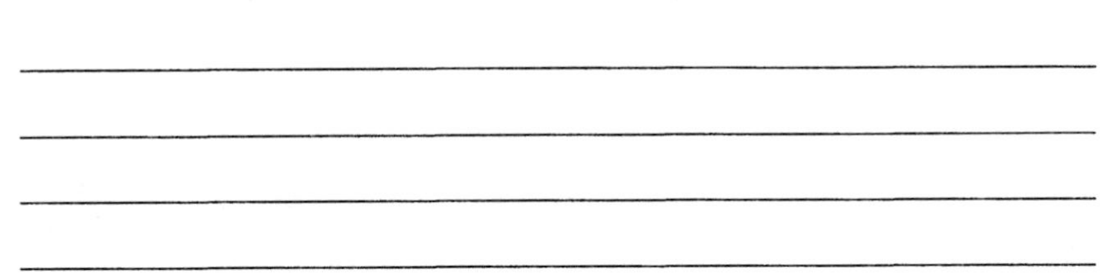

Worksheet 6.5. Relationship with Mother

1. Rate the degree of emotional closeness between you and your mother before age 15:

0	1	2	3	4	5	6	7	8	9	10
Not Close					Moderately Close					Very Close

Describe your relationship with your mother before age 15 (discuss sense of closeness, emotional connection, intimacy, emotional boundaries, affection):

2. Rate the degree of emotional closeness between you and your mother today:

0	1	2	3	4	5	6	7	8	9	10
Not Close					Moderately Close					Very Close

Describe your relationship with your mother today (discuss sense of closeness, emotional connection, intimacy, emotional boundaries, affection):

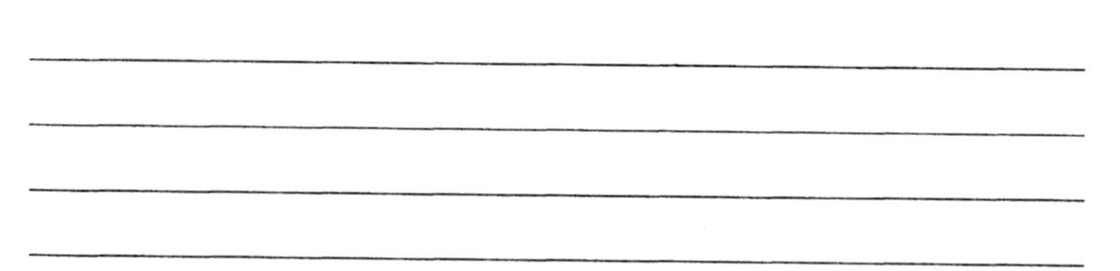

Worksheet 6.6. What Did You Learn?

Directions: Think back to your parents and to others who may have taught you important lessons about what it means to be a man and a woman. Identify what you learned from these sources through what they said, did not say, did, or did not do.

From Your Father Growing Up	
About what it means to be a man...	*About what it means to be a woman...*
From Your Mother Growing Up	
About what it means to be a man...	*About what it means to be a woman...*
From ________________ (e.g., church, media, TV, movies, friends)	
About what it means to be a man...	*About what it means to be a woman...*

Worksheet 6.7. Looking for Closeness

Directions: Consider somebody (a non-family member of the same sex) in your life with whom you would like to feel a greater sense of emotional connection or closeness. Please rate your (a) desire to connect emotionally with that person, (b) degree to which you feel fascinated (or compelled to connect) with this person, and (c) extent to which you experience a sexually charged fascination with this person.

A. Desire to connect emotionally with ________________.

0 1 2 3 4 5 6 7 8 9 10

No Desire   Somewhat of a Desire   Strong Desire

Describe:

____

____

B. Degree to which I feel fascinated (or compelled to connect) with __________.

0 1 2 3 4 5 6 7 8 9 10

Not Compelled   Somewhat Compelled   Very Compelled

Describe:

____

____

C. Extent to which I experience sexually charged fascination with ___________.

0 1 2 3 4 5 6 7 8 9 10

None   Moderate   Very Strong

Describe:

____

____

Chapter

7

Living a Practical Theology of Sanctification

Understanding Sanctification

Have you ever tried to follow a diet? Perhaps you have tried cutting out sweets for a time, or maybe you have avoided carbohydrates for a few weeks. Maybe you tried eating one meal a day. Although you may have heard about dozens of new diets that will "do the trick," you may have become somewhat cynical that there is any one fixed program that really works for you. In other words you may have begun to realize that there is no such thing as a "trick" when it comes to successful dieting.

Most nutritional experts today are in consensus that people take the best care of themselves when they say "no" to a fad diet and say "yes" to a lifestyle change. A diet suggests something formulaic—that there is a simple formula you can follow to "shed the pounds." A lifestyle change suggests that all of the things that make up your life need to be re-examined in light of your goal of taking care of your body. In one sense, this is harder. It is much more of a longstanding commitment than simply skipping meals or cutting out carbs. But it is easier in the sense that once you have re-worked your life to take care of your body, you find a rhythm in living consistently these new patterns. That does not mean you are free from temptation or from occasional setbacks, but it does mean that exceptions may be made to a daily and weekly routine that places your health before your impulses to eat whatever you like whenever you like.

The approach that we are presenting in this book is not a "program" you follow for a few weeks or a few months. As we consider the last major piece of what we have found to be most helpful for people who contend with same-sex attraction and behavior and seek change, we want to note that we are advocating a *process* rather than a program. We are talking more about the trajectory your life is on rather than a few weeks or months of encouraging you to do things differently.

This will become increasingly clear to you as we introduce the concept of *sanctification*, since in many ways the culmination of sanctification (that is, glorification) is experienced in eternity. As you will see, as we are sanctified we find that our relationships are increasingly characterized by shalom (justice and peace). People do not quickly pull together relationships characterized by shalom. But we will make the case that eternity begins in the here-and-now, and that you can intentionally place your life in the context of God's plan for who He sees you as today, as well as who He sees you as in light of eternity. First, let us unpack the implications of sanctification; then we will turn to the concept of shalom.

A Practical Theology of Sanctification

What is a practical theology of sanctification? This is essentially a concrete way to think about what God is doing in your life. It is *practical* because we focus on concrete ways to grow as a person, to think and behave in relationships. It is a practical *theology of sanctification* because we are talking about what it means to live faithfully before God in light of ongoing experiences of same-sex attraction. Sanctification is a Christian concept that refers to what it means to be made holy; it is the process of being "set apart" for God's purposes. People who are drawn to this understanding are essentially resolving to live their lives with reference to beliefs and values consistent with what they believe and perhaps what their religion—in this case Christianity—has historically taught about God's intentions for sexual behavior. In the case of Christianity, that teaching is fidelity in heterosexual marriage or celibacy outside of marriage.

If this describes your personal conviction, you are not alone. There have been many Christians from the Roman Catholic, Orthodox, and evangelical communities, for example, who have been ordering their internal and external lives and "faithfully dealing with their desires for the same sex according to the plain teaching of Scripture."[1] In this context, it is especially important to hear the voices of Christians who experience same-sex attraction and have experienced these circumstances as a means by which God has provided His grace and mercy.

Let us emphasize that this is not a question of denying oneself enjoyment or pleasure; that could not be further from the truth from a Christian perspective. But the measures of desire and pleasure being offered up for us today are hardly the things of which Christianity consists. We can desire and hope for peace and enjoyment, but of what sort? C. S. Lewis, in *The Weight of Glory*, notes that

> ...it would seem that Our Lord finds our desires not too strong, but too weak. We are half-hearted creatures, fooling around with drink and sex and ambition when infinite joy is offered us, like an ignorant child who wants to go on making mud pies in a slum because he cannot imagine what is meant by the offer of a holiday at sea. We are far too easily pleased.[2]

Critics might say, "There goes another Christian promising the rewards of a future life but denying the pleasures of this life." But that is a mischaracterization of Lewis' worldview. As Lewis noted, the fact that heaven awaits the Christian is not "simply tacked on to the activity" of obedient living, for example, but rewards are "the activity itself in consummation."[3] He continues:

> Those who have attained everlasting life in the vision of God doubtless know very well that it is no mere bribe, but the very consummation of their earthly discipleship; but we who have not yet attained it cannot know this in the same way, and cannot even begin to know it at all except by continuing to obey and finding the reward of our obedience in our increasing power to desire the ultimate reward.[4]

In other words, the entire context of the Christian life is with reference to eternity. It is not as though we muddle through this life and then delight in the glories of heaven when we die. Rather, all that we do in this lifetime as discipleship—which includes obedience to the Christian sexual ethic as best we are able by the grace of God through the Holy Spirit—is a part of what we continue to enjoy in its full consummation in heaven.

So what is our *activity* and what is its *consummation*? Our *activity* is obedience, discipleship, and sanctification. That is, being made more and more in the likeness of Christ. And our *consummation* is to be fully Christ-like in the glorification that awaits us in heaven.

From a Christian perspective, practical emphasis might be placed on developing what Dallas Willard refers to as a "curriculum of Christ-likeness."[5] You may have seen people wearing bracelets with the letters, WWJD? They stand for *What Would Jesus Do?* This phrase is related to what Willard writes about when he refers to a curriculum of Christ-likeness, but, as Willard observes, the answer to the question, *What Would Jesus Do?* can only be answered with reference to how Jesus lived. From this perspective the question is not *What Would Jesus Do?* but *How Did Jesus Live?* This is the essential basis for a curriculum of Christ-likeness and it involves two key elements:

1) Clearly positioning the context before the heavenly Father's present rule through Jesus, and
2) Walking the individual through actual cases in their own lives to give them experienced-based understanding and assurance.[6]

The first of these two key elements is concerned with seeing one's circumstances accurately, and from a Christian perspective, this means seeing one's circumstances in the context of God's redemptive plan. This first element succinctly captures what we have been discussing so far: if you are interested in living your life faithfully before God as you understand the Christian sexual ethic, then you must see your life—your present circumstances, challenges, temptations, setbacks, victories, and so on—from the vantage point of God's sovereign rule of all that He has created.

The second of the key elements is a call for friends and family (and in some cases professional counselors or paraprofessional support groups) to walk alongside you in your experiences of same-sex attraction. Willard's writing also reflects appreciation for and the prescription of the use of classic spiritual disciplines to help live out this curriculum. These disciplines include active involvement in corporate worship, prayer, fasting, solitude, service, and the like. As we consider spiritual disciplines in the context of our approach, we would say that the incorporation of spiritual disciplines is not to change orientation as such (although that may happen by God's grace and power), but that the spiritual disciplines "are practices that change the inner self and its relationship to the 'helper' (*paraclete*), so that we actually can do what we would and avoid what we would not."[7]

This brings us to the work of the Holy Spirit. If you agree with what Dallas Willard is saying about the spiritual life, then you might agree that the function of the Holy Spirit is "to move within our souls, and especially our minds, to present the person of Jesus and the reality of his kingdom."[8] If you are a Christian, then, the Holy Spirit plays an active and vital role in shaping your inner life and the acts that come to reflect the nature of that inner life.

This approach is nothing new. It is consistent with what the church has historically taught about self-discipline. This perspective obviously carries with it an appreciation for one's future. If one's future is found in a closed system of cause and effect, and if it merely reflects what we have accumulated by the end of our lives, then it is no surprise that an approach that incorporates self-discipline is intolerable. But if people see their lives laid before them—in the present life and in the future—both of which are properly understood as the Kingdom of God according to Willard, then we will live in anticipation of the culmination and re-formation of the world and of ourselves, and this will have immediate relevance to how we live today.

The following suggested activities build on this understanding and are intended to help you develop a spiritual foundation and sensitivity to developing a practical theology of sanctification.

Areas of Struggle

Consider reflecting first on your unique areas of struggle. Mark's colleague, Michael Mangis, refers to these as "signature sins." This is the pattern of struggle with sin that is unique to you. You may be thinking, "Well, that's obvious. I struggle with homosexual thoughts and behaviors." Okay, fair enough. But rather than think narrowly about your struggles with sexual attractions and behaviors, think more broadly about your struggles. Think about how each of us struggles with different experiences. Some of us struggle more with a combination of anger, irritation, and impatience. Others struggle more with a combination of pride and envy. Still others may struggle with a mix of lust and sloth. What would you say characterizes your unique struggle? What are your signature sins?

One way you might begin to answer this question is to read portions of Saint Augustine's *Prayer Book*, where he discusses the seven deadly sins. Each of the seven deadly sins is further divided into other specific sins that a person may struggle with. As you read over this material, ask God to help you further your understanding of your unique struggle. As you begin to sort this out look for clusters of sins where some have a special kind of intensity or frequency for you.

To help you sort through these issues further, buy a journal and begin to take note of your signature sins and your reaction to what you find as you complete this reading and other related readings. Then begin to answer the following questions: *What stands out to you as you review your responses to your readings? Do you notice any themes (are any of the areas of struggle related)? Describe your history of struggling in these areas? What have you done in the past to address these areas?* and *How is what you see related to your life goals?*

Covetousness

One specific area of struggle cited by some people who experience same-sex attraction and pursue change is covetousness. This may seem surprising to you, and covetousness is not a word many people are familiar with, so let's take some time to better understand the experience itself. Covetousness "is a form of distorted, misplaced, or unlawful desire focused on another's possessions or property, or even another person."[9] It is the experience of desiring for yourself qualities you find in others. With homosexual attractions, some people who experience same-sex attraction report a strong, misplaced desire for the qualities or characteristics of others of their same sex. For example, Sam reported coveting the masculine characteristics he saw in other men, including their physical build, confidence, or assertiveness. He discovered that these qualities drew him to other men, and he believed this was an experience of covetousness that played a significant role in his experiences of same-sex attraction.

You may or may not experience this kind of covetousness. If you do, use Worksheet 7.1 to begin to unpack the meaning of your experiences by identifying qualities or characteristics of others of the same sex that you have wanted for yourself. Again, this may not be your experience, but if it is, it may be a real struggle for you. You may also have a longing for qualities in others but you may not have ever thought of it as covetousness. We do not want you to get tripped up on the wording. We have heard others describe this as a desire to cannibalize others—to take in the qualities that you may feel are missing in yourself. In the context of our discussion of a practical theology of sanctification, we prefer the term covetousness mainly because of the spiritual connotations of missing the mark as you may struggle with not feeling like you have all of the qualities or characteristics you may wish you had.

As you begin to reflect on the qualities or characteristics you may covet in others, begin to identify the constraints that keep you from changing in this area, and begin to consider strategies for removing those constraints. Remember our previous discussion of Albert and his identification of constraints and possible solutions? If you need a refresher in identifying and removing constraints, you may turn back to this section in Chapter 5.

Toward Fidelity

A concept that is often related to sanctification, especially for people struggling with sexual issues, is fidelity. This word fidelity refers to *faithfulness*. This is the kind of faithfulness you have to your marriage, vocation (a calling), friendships, and God, among other things. But fidelity is more than static faithfulness; it involves creativity and investment, so that our ongoing relationships and vocations are continuously re-created and renewed.[10]

Read through a story about faithfulness in Scripture. It is found in Hosea 2:21-22, and take a few minutes to reflect on God's fidelity to His people. After you read this story, use Worksheet 7.2 to begin to consider who or what you are called to be faithful to, including God, your spouse (if you are married), children (if you have children), and so on. To help you unpack the practical implications of fidelity for you, you might begin by thinking of it as a real thing, an object in the room that you can point to and reflect on: What demands is fidelity making of you right now in the areas you mentioned, such as your relationship with your spouse? What has made achieving greater fidelity difficult for you in these areas? In other words, we assume that achieving fidelity is difficult and that you have faced a number of things (internal or external) that function as constraints. What, then, are other ways you can address these constraints by thinking about "creative fidelity" or the continuous re-creating or renewing of your faithfulness in specific relationships?

Toward Chastity

Another important word is chastity. *Chastity* involves being faithful to God's intention for human sexuality and sexual behavior, including fidelity in marriage and celibacy outside of marriage. Chastity is "the morally responsible exercise of human sexuality in the human community. To be chaste is to be morally blameless, to treat with honor, respect, troth and integrity ourselves and our neighbors as persons, image-bearers of God.... [Chastity is] the purity of heart and integrity of person which we owe to ourselves and each other as children of God, called to do everything in the name of love."[11]

As you begin to consider what it means to live a chaste life, use Worksheet 7.3 and try to identify three things that would need to be changed in order for you to live a more chaste life. What keeps you from making specific changes in order for you to experience chastity? Again, these things that get in the way function as constraints. Begin to reflect on specific strategies that would help you to overcome these specific constraints.

Forgiveness

Another significant step in a practical theology of sanctification is to receive forgiveness and to give it freely to others. Forgiveness is "the mutual recognition that repentance of either or both parties is genuine and that right relationships have been restored or achieved. The three requirements of forgiveness are: the restoration of an attitude of love, the working through of pain, anger, and alienation, and the opening of the future to appropriate relating...."[12] The first two dimensions of forgiveness are perhaps the most crucial, that is, to have a restored attitude of love toward the person who is being forgiven and to work through negative emotions that make forgiveness difficult. Opening yourself up to a future relationship refers to reconciliation.

Reflect on the definition of forgiveness above. Where are you in the process of forgiving yourself? Using Worksheet 7.4, begin to identify three things that would need to be changed for you to forgive yourself. What are the specific things that make forgiving yourself especially difficult? Identify those things that function as constraints to forgiveness. What specific strategies can you work on to help remove those constraints?

Let's take a look at an example of forgiving ourselves. Mary, seeking accountability from Lori, would meet with her weekly to discuss issues related to her experiences with same-sex attractions and behaviors. On one particular week, Mary opened the discussion by reporting that she was angry with herself. "How could I do this again?" Mary repeated to herself. She was obviously quite upset about a recent sexual encounter she had with a friend. When asked if she had sought forgiveness from God and herself, Mary said, "How can I forgive myself; I knew better?"

While talking with Mary, Lori helped her identify a number of her thoughts that made it difficult for Mary to forgive herself, such as, "I should have known better." "I knew what I was doing, and I didn't stop myself." "I wanted to have sex with her." Some of the specific things that made it difficult for Mary to forgive herself came out during the conversation. From Mary's standpoint, because she engaged in sex with a friend, she was responsible not only for her sin but for her friend's sin. Her position in a local ministry also made it difficult for Mary to forgive herself.

Working with Mary to remove the constraints impeding her from forgiving herself took some time. Mary acknowledged that she was experiencing internal conflict regarding her behavior. There was a "part" of her who knew it was wrong, but also a "part" of her who enjoyed the intimacy she experienced through her behavior. Charting out her thoughts and feeling about forgiveness helped Mary to see that she was embracing irrational thinking, which was leading to shame and condemnation about who she was as a person. Mary described herself in all-or-nothing terms. "I am a sicko. How can I be a child of God too?" Mary was able to forgive herself in the end and learn from mapping out the patterns and activities that led to the sexual encounters with her friend. Mary's experience certainly brings to light some of the many challenges people face as they consider what it means to forgive themselves and accept God's forgiveness.

Now revisit the definition of forgiveness and consider what it would mean to forgive someone close to you. For some people this is a parent—your father or mother. For others this is a sibling or other family member. It may also be a spouse. You may be struggling with forgiving a close friend, pastor, neighbor, or co-worker. Where are you in the process of forgiving these friends or family members? Begin to identify three things that would need to be changed for you to forgive a specific person. Identify those things that function as constraints to your ability to make these changes. What strategies would help you remove those constraints?

Let's consider another example. Helen entered therapy determined to save her marriage. Her husband was recently arrested for solicitation in a male bathroom of a local shopping mall. This was the second time Jim had been arrested in the last two years. According to Helen, she forgave him the first time, but did not know if she could forgive him again. Helen found it hard to speak to Jim in a "civil" tongue. She often found herself yelling insults at him during arguments and struggling with feelings of contempt and anger. She wanted to "do the right thing" and forgive Jim. She believed this to be her "Christian" duty.

What keeps Helen from forgiving Jim? What would happen if she forgave him? These were questions Helen struggled to answer as she worked through difficult thoughts and feelings. She wondered what her parents would say if she forgave him. "Jim knew better." "He made promises to me that this would never happen again." Helen also struggled with issues related to her femininity that kept her in destructive patterns of thinking and relating. "What is wrong with me as a woman?" "Why would Jim want someone else?" I must not satisfy him." "I deserve more than from him."

Helen, like many others, struggled with forgiveness. Remember, forgiveness is not the same as condoning or accepting behaviors. So, it is not an issue of Helen condoning or accepting Jim's behaviors. Identifying the place where she was at in her process of forgiving Jim and the constraints that made it difficult for her to work through forgiveness afforded Helen a new perspective on her situation. She began to systematically examine her thoughts and feelings fueling her unforgiveness. Eventually, Helen was able to identify the things that she believed needed changing for her to forgive Jim and the strategies that might her help in this process. Some of the strategies were as simple as taking a "time out" when she felt her heart begin to beat faster while in a discussion with Jim.

Prayer

Prayer is also a significant resource from the perspective of a practical theology of sanctification. Prayer is your conversation with God. There are many approaches to prayer, and we simply invite you to make prayer an ongoing part of a practical theology of sanctification. One way to begin is to think of your time in prayer as having four parts: praising God, confessing areas and instances of struggle, giving thanks, and asking for help. Begin by praising God for who He is. You might focus here on God's attributes, such as His goodness and kindness, or God's faithfulness and compassion.

Next, reflect on the areas of struggle you have been identifying in your life. These are the broad "signature sins" you are becoming familiar with, and this is also a time to confess specific instances of struggle. For example, you might find that you can confess a "signature sin" that involves self-centeredness, pride, and covetousness. Perhaps this is your signature cluster of sins. You can also confess a specific instance if, for example, you recently focused too much on yourself in an exchange with a friend and missed an opportunity to be a loving, supportive presence in your friend's life. In this part of prayer you are essentially confessing the ways in which you have fallen short of God's desire for you.

Then spend time thanking God for the many things He has given you. For some people these things may include personal health, employment, family relationships, a local community of friends, and so on. This is a sensitive area, of course, and we recognize that you may have ongoing struggles in certain relationships. Perhaps your parents have rejected you because you disclosed to them that you experience same-sex attraction. It may be beneficial to you to make a decision to thank God for the people in your life, even if those people are not relating to you in a way that is God's desire for you. That is a point you can make as you ask God to help bring about restored relationships, but for the present it is important to express genuine gratitude for all that God has given you.

Finally, let God know your needs and also pray for the needs of others. Identify any answers to your prayers, as it is important to remember God's faithfulness to answer us when we pray.

Having unpacked our understanding of sanctification and the practical implications for those who contend with same-sex attraction, we turn now to the concept of shalom. We said earlier that our experience of sanctification should increase our experience of shalom. But we need to examine more closely what this means and begin to identify the practical strategies for cultivating relationships characterized by shalom.

Living in Shalom

Shalom is a Hebraic word that has to do with enjoying relationships that are characterized by justice and peace. In his book *Until Justice and Peace Embrace*, Christian philosopher Nicolas Wolterstorff defines shalom as being able to flourish in your relationships, to take delight in relationships with yourself, others, God, and your physical surroundings.[13] It is more than merely freedom from conflict, as when two nations co-exist during a time of peace. In the Middle East today there is great conflict among several nations, to take a contemporary example. But even if peace negotiations were to succeed in a ceasefire, would we say that these nations live in shalom? No, a ceasefire may end violence (which is a negative account of how these nations relate), but it does not necessarily promote shalom (a positive account of how nations can relate). In other words, nations do not live in shalom simply because they are free from war; rather, their experience of shalom is related to their ability to truly flourish in their relationship as nations. The same is true for your relationships. Whether we are speaking of your relationship with yourself, others, or God, the fact that you are not in open conflict with another or yourself does not mean that you are experiencing shalom.

Let us now consider what it means to live in shalom as it pertains to your concerns about experiencing or acting on same-sex attractions.

Yourself

Many people who experience same-sex attraction and want to experience a change struggle with delighting in relation to themselves. Critics of the Christian sexual ethic say, "Of course you fail to delight in relation to yourself because you are not being honest with yourself, because you are not 'coming out' as having a gay identity." Recall, however, that you are more than the sum of your experiences of same-sex attraction, and that ours is the only culture and the only time throughout history in which people make the self-defining attribution, "I am gay." Recall also that you are being honest with yourself that you have experiences of same-sex attraction. You are not in denial about this, but you are choosing to live a chaste life in response to your particular attractions so that your behaviors are congruent with your beliefs and values about God's intention for human sexuality.

At the same time we want to acknowledge that some people who experience same-sex attraction genuinely struggle with their sense of self-worth. Although they may feel guilt for specific behaviors and may request and receive forgiveness for distinct acts of disobedience, they may struggle with a deeper sense of personal shame. This shame has to do with experiencing same-sex attractions as who one is as a person. If you believe that your same-sex attractions reflect who you are as a person, then you may struggle greatly with shame if you hold to a Christian sexual ethic about same-sex behavior. In other words, if you struggle with this, you may find you are more likely to find yourself condemning not just discrete acts but your entire *self.*

If this reflects your struggle, we have some words of encouragement to share with you. In our experience, people do not choose to experience same-sex attraction. In all of our years of counseling we have yet to come across someone who made the choice to begin to experience same-sex attraction. Rather, most people who struggle in this area simply just find themselves experiencing homosexual attractions. As you probably are aware, some self-identifying gay persons use this fact to argue for the morality of same-sex behavior. They argue that since people do not choose their attractions, they cannot be morally responsible for acting upon them. This reasoning is flawed, however. You probably know a great number of people who have feelings they never chose but who must decide what to do with those feelings. So while we disagree with those who say that homosexual behavior is a good thing since people do not choose to experience same-sex attraction, we believe that this fact gives us great empathy for those who contend with same-sex attraction. Among those feelings or attractions that people might contend with, surely same-sex attraction is among the most difficult.

So God's moral standard does not change, but neither does God's love for you. It seems to us that God is clearly and radically identifying with you in your humanity, and that God wants to meet you where you are, even if where you are is currently experiencing same-sex attraction. These attractions may not reflect God's intention for human sexuality or sexual expression, but the attractions were not chosen by you, and you need not identify with them nor feel shame for their very existence. As we have noted, the reasons for the existence of same-sex attractions vary from person to person, and may involve several factors weighted differently for different persons. None of this points to factors that you ought to feel shame about. If you have willingly participated in same-sex behavior as an adult, then there may be behaviors for which you may need to seek forgiveness, but these are discrete acts that are quite different from the attractions themselves. Even if these discrete acts have occurred in serial relationships over the course of several years, they are still within earshot of God's gracious voice.

It is our opinion that if your homosexual attractions persist, you need not seek God's forgiveness for experiencing them, unless you are convinced that you are doing things to facilitate those attractions. While many people are ambivalent about their same-sex attractions (for example, seeking out ways to facilitate them through fantasy. while often feeling guilt about such actions), few who pursue a course of change seek them out in the same way as those who are taking on a gay or lesbian identity.

There are other things you can do to help address your tendency to experience shame. Many of these things revolve around developing a supportive network of mature friends and growing in your relationship with God, so we will turn to these areas insofar as God intends them to be relationships characterized by shalom.

Others

There are obvious connections between what it means to delight in relationship with oneself and with others. Indeed, many people believe you must accept yourself before you can adequately love another. But in contemporary terms, this so often translates into a rather thin view of love. More often than not, such an understanding amounts to essentially self-actualization, which in contemporary terms is thin because it has very little to do with actualizing the self God intends for you to be. In its place we find a kind of egoism, a focus on the self and its pleasures, so that people essentially pursue those things that bring them pleasure and avoid those things that bring them pain. But the word shalom will challenge you to delight in relationship with yourself, others, and God, such that your self-actualization is the actualizing of your potential for relating to others through God's eyes. It is what God sees as His best for you with respect to your relationships.

Indeed, with respect to your experiences of same-sex attraction, much of what we have been writing about thus far has focused on achieving and maintaining chastity in relationships with others. Although this may be a door that opens in on shalom, it is not shalom in and of itself. But how can chastity be in any way related to self-actualization? Isn't chastity a negative thing? Isn't it depriving me of sexual intimacy? In truth, in all or nearly all the relationships you have today, chastity is everyone's goal whose goal it is to live faithfully before God and in relation to His revealed will about sexual ethics. But we do the Christian sexual ethic an injustice if we define chastity negatively. A proper understanding of chastity requires a proper understanding of the word *love*.

To understand the meaning of the word love, we need to take a slight detour to Alaska. We need to discuss snow. Did you know that it's been said that some Inuit persons in Alaska have over 17 names for snow? Because snow is a part of the lives of Inuit persons more so than most of us can imagine, they are familiar enough with snow that they "see" many different variations in texture that most people do not see. No one would expect Native Americans to import an understanding of snow from somewhere in Tennessee, Virginia, or California. Indeed, we could learn more about snow from them.

Something similar happens when we think about the meaning of the word love. Unfortunately, most people in our culture today equate love with sex. They speak of "making love" through sexual intercourse. But what they have done is taken several variations of love and reduced them to only one such expression—genital sexual activity—it is no wonder people feel "deprived" of love by a "narrow" Christian sexual ethic that proscribes sexual behavior outside of marriage. If sexual behavior is the only or primary expression of what it means to give and receive love, then genital sexual activity takes on special importance as a *right* reflecting what it means to be truly human.

But Christians have access to an understanding of love that far surpasses this thin definition. In fact, love has been defined in no fewer than four ways in the Greek:

Eros. The first word we want to consider is *eros*. This is a word that reflects a kind of desire to possess another, and it also captures a longing for union with another, an affectionate desire to connect. It is from the word *eros* that we get the word erotic. Because our culture focuses in narrowly on sexual behaviors as expressions of love we probably think more often about love and intimacy as associated most closely with genital sexual expression.

Storge. An alternative to *eros* is *storge*, a Greek word for love that connotes something about affection among family members. This family love is seen as a mother cares for an infant.

Phileo. A very common word for love in Scripture is *phileo.* This is love experienced between friends. *Phileo* is seen most often experienced through friendly affection, and it reflects an expression of care and regard for others in their struggles. You may have good friends who you connect with, and this kind of meaningful, truly fulfilling love may be overlooked in the present focus on erotic sex.

Agape. The last Greek word and the most commonly used word for love in Scripture is *agape.* This love is characterized by self-sacrifice; it reflects a posture of giving in relation to another, where the person loved has not merited the love. Agape love seeks the highest good in another person. If you love a person with agape love, you want what is best for them, and you love in a giving, sacrificial way. In fact, the nature of God is what is often used to define agape love—that is, God is love, as we read in 1 John 4:8. What love we enjoy in human terms is made available because of who God is.

The purpose of this short lesson in Greek is to simply help you understand that there are many ways to think about and express love, care, and intimacy in your relationships with others. Like so many people influenced by our broader culture, perhaps you have foreclosed prematurely on your understanding of love and have limited its expression to only those specific sexual acts that supposedly communicate or express love, as is implied in the popular phrase "making love." Not only is this phrase a misleading claim for all sexual experiences, but it is a distortion of what it means to experience and communicate love in relation to oneself, others, and God.

God

Just as it is difficult for people who experience same-sex attractions to feel at peace with themselves because of shame, and with others because of a narrow understanding of what it means to give and receive love, it can be extraordinarily difficult to feel at peace in relationship with God. Again, it is not that people feel God cannot or will not forgive them for specific instances of sin. Many people struggle with specific areas and seek and receive forgiveness for these struggles. But what we are thinking of here is a willingness to be accepted by God for who a person is, even if that person is someone who continues to experience same-sex attraction, perhaps despite a few years in counseling or therapy. Is there room in this discussion to experience peace in one's relationship with God while experiencing ongoing struggles with same-sex attraction? Yes.

How do we get there? Begin by putting same-sex attractions in perspective. From a Christian perspective, all of our struggles with desires that run counter to God's intention for us are simply reflections of our fallen condition. When we act on those desires, we are morally responsible for our behaviors. In this context, behaviors include lustful thoughts and actual behaviors. Same-sex thoughts or attractions can lead to a sinful response, that is, lustful thoughts and actual behaviors. So you are not morally culpable for the fact that you experience same-sex thoughts or attractions. Neither is a woman who struggles with sexual attractions beyond her marriage morally responsible for thoughts about or attractions to other men. But she is responsible for whether she lusts after other men or engages in an emotional or sexual affair with other men.

So in placing your experiences of same-sex attraction in context, you see that you are not alone. You belong to a category of people—in fact, all of humanity —struggling with one or more reflections of our fallen condition. The fact that your local church or the broader Christian community may make it out to be an especially shameful or egregious struggle does not change the fact that we all miss the mark in one way or another, and that each of us is constituted in such a way that we struggle with propensities to sin in specific ways. You may actually play a role in helping the Christian community see its responsibility to Christians who contend with same-sex attraction and are trying to live faithfully before God in the context of their local church community. In our opinion, the way the church has responded (or failed to respond) to those in its midst who contend with same-sex attraction has probably led people to foreclose on what the church has to offer them and to enter into the gay community as the only viable alternative they perceive as open to them in light of their present struggles.

Reflections on Living a Practical Theology of Sanctification

1. How does thinking about your struggles in the context of your personal sanctification change how you view your experiences of same-sex attraction? Although you may not ever know for certain this side of heaven, what do you suppose God may be doing with you in light of these struggles?
2. Think about what it means for you to delight in your relationship with yourself. What comes to your mind? How is "delighting in yourself" as discussed in this chapter different from being selfish or even self-focused?
3. What does it mean to delight in your relationship with others? Have you thought about different types of love before? How has this chapter expanded your understanding of various expressions of love?
4. Think about your relationship with God. Do you delight in your relationship with Him? What about your current struggles has made it difficult to delight in God? What are some of the things that you would want to have in place for you to delight more in your relationship with God?
5. What can you teach your local church and the broader Christian community about what it means to live courageously and faithfully before God?

Worksheet 7.1. Covetousness

Covetousness "is a form of distorted, misplaced or unlawful desire focused on another's possessions or property, or even another person (Ex. 20:17; Dt. 5:21)." [14] Some people who experience same-sex attraction report a strong, misplaced desire for the qualities or characteristics of others of their same sex.

Identify any qualities or characteristics of others of the same sex that you have wanted for yourself:

Person:	*Quality or Characteristic:*
Person:	*Quality or Characteristic:*

Do you see any connection between this desire for these qualities and your experiences of same-sex attraction and/or behavior? Explain:

____

____

Identify the constraints that keep you from appreciating the qualities you have, developing these qualities further, and appreciating the qualities in others for what they are:

1. ______________________________________

2. ______________________________________

Identify strategies that would help you overcome these constraints:

1. ______________________________________

2. ______________________________________

Worksheet 7.2. Toward Fidelity[15]

Fidelity refers to faithfulness to marriage, vocation (a calling), friendships, and God, among other things. But fidelity is more than static faithfulness; it involves creativity and investment, so that our ongoing relationships and vocations are continuously renewed.

Read Hosea 2:21-22. Describe God's fidelity to His people:

____

God is faithful to His vow, and God is faithful to His commitment to the well-being of His people.

What/who do you believe you are called to be faithful to?

- ☐ God
- ☐ Your local church/religious community
- ☐ Husband or wife
- ☐ A station or calling (be specific): _______
- ☐ Singleness
- ☐ Your child/children
- ☐ Other (be specific): ______________________________

What demands is fidelity making of you in the area(s) you selected above?

____

What has made achieving greater fidelity difficult for you in the area(s) above?

____

Identify constraint(s):

____

What ways can you pursue creative fidelity (a continuously re-created and renewed relationship or vocation) in the area(s) above?

____

Worksheet 7.3. Toward Chastity

Chastity involves being faithful to God's intention for human sexuality and sexual behavior, including fidelity in marriage and celibacy outside of marriage. Chastity is "the morally responsible exercise of human sexuality in the human community. To be chaste is to be morally blameless, to treat with honor, respect, troth, and integrity to ourselves and our neighbors as persons, image-bearers of God.... [Chastity is] the purity of heart and integrity of person which we owe to ourselves and each other as children of God, called to do everything in the name of love."[16]

What are the three things that would need to be changed for you to live more of a chaste life?

1. ______________________________

2. ______________________________

3. ______________________________

What keeps you from changing each of these three things?

1. ______________________________

2. ______________________________

Identify constraint(s):

____

Identify strategies that could help you overcome these constraints:

1. ______________________________

2. ______________________________

3. ______________________________

Worksheet 7.4. Forgiveness

Forgiveness means to "put aside," "send away," or "let go" of an offense. From a theological perspective, forgiveness is based on the experience Christians have of God forgiving them following repentance (a turning away) from their sins. Because of God's mercy in forgiving us, we are called by God to forgive others. This is true even if the person who offends us does not ask for forgiveness or believe that he or she needs to be forgiven. Forgiveness does not mean that we put ourselves in the position to be hurt again, but it does recognize that we (and those who have hurt us) have fallen short of God's intention for our lives.

What are the three things that would need to be changed for you to forgive?

1. ____________________

2. ____________________

3. ____________________

What keeps you from changing each of these three things?

1. ____________________

2. ____________________

Identify constraint(s):

____

Identify strategies that would help you overcome these constraints:

1. ____________________

2. ____________________

3. ____________________

Part 3:

Serving the Image of God in All Persons

Chapter 8

A Word to Families

The focus of this book has been to provide a practical resource to those who experience unwanted same-sex attractions. But people who contend with same-sex attraction do not do so in a vacuum. They experience same-sex attraction and struggle, often in isolation, but in the context of a larger community, their family, and the church. So we turn our attention to those who are affected when someone shares his or her struggles with same-sex attraction. These include family members, especially parents and spouses, and the broader community of faith, the church.

The most typical expression of concern comes from parents, siblings, and spouses of loved ones who experience same-sex attraction. If you are a parent, let's look at some of your specific concerns.

Parents

James and Amanda requested counseling for their son, Scott, age 15. James and Amanda requested help because Scott had recently revealed to them that he was experiencing same-sex attractions. James stated that when Scott first disclosed this information, he felt "concerned" and "disappointed." James clarified that he was not disappointed in Scott *as a person*, but that hearing that his son was experiencing same-sex attraction and might be gay was so far from what he envisioned for his son. It was presented as a kind of loss for James. James noted that Scott had taken pride in being "different" in his dress and music, and so he thought that the ways in which Scott was different related to those expressions, not to experiences of same-sex attraction.

Amanda had a stronger negative reaction to Scott's disclosure. She insisted that James contact a local mental health professional to "get help" for Scott, who she saw as needing to change his orientation. She was much more upset by Scott's experiences of same-sex attraction and came across to Scott as blaming him for his experiences, as though she were saying, "If you weren't trying to be so 'different,' you wouldn't have these problems."

Being parents, like James and Amanda, you may be concerned that your son or daughter just announced that he or she struggles with same-sex attraction. Or perhaps your child does not "struggle" at all, but has embraced the experiences and is taking on a gay or lesbian identity. Perhaps you are concerned that your child has foreclosed prematurely on other options. There are no easy answers, but we want to share with you a few principles, and then illustrate the application of these principles through various examples.

Listen, Listen, Listen

The place to begin is to listen to your son or daughter. If your child is experiencing same-sex attraction, feels shame and fear about that, and is concerned about whether you would reject them, listen to their fears. Listen for their story, and provide your child with assurances of your love, followed by actions that clearly reinforce what you have verbally communicated.

In the above scenario, what seemed to help this family was encouraging James and Amanda to listen to Scott, and to help them be honest with Scott about their fears for him. Listening was especially difficult for Amanda, but James was willing to spend several sessions hearing about Scott's experiences and perspectives on how his faith as a Christian was related to his sexual behavior. Both James and Amanda worked on being honest with Scott about their fears for him. They wanted him to be able to marry and have children. James was particularly sensitive to whether Scott would be ostracized or stigmatized by others, especially if, down the road, he were to pursue a same-sex relationship. Scott's experience of same-sex attraction evoked a negative reaction from his parents, in part because they struggled with anticipatory grief and loss for fears that had not yet been expressed, and these fears had to do with his future, whether he would marry, whether he would have children, and whether they would have grandchildren. Listening, coupled with honesty, our next principle, can help this family and perhaps yours successfully navigate through a difficult course.

Be Honest

It is important that you are honest about what you find particularly challenging. Challenges can come in all shapes and sizes. If your child is distressed by his or her experiences of same-sex attraction, you can join with your child in an honest account of their circumstances. Listen, yes, and share your perspective on sexuality, sexual identity, and sexual behavior. But keep in mind that your child did not set out to experience same-sex attraction. While there may be many things your child can do to decrease the intensity, frequency, and duration of same-sex attractions, your child did not choose to experience the attractions, and that can translate into greater empathy for their circumstances on your part.

Honesty is always important, and it can be especially difficult if your child has embraced a gay identity in such a way that you find yourself locking horns over beliefs and values. For example, your daughter may want to bring her partner to visit during a school break. You may struggle with whether your daughter will understand if you say that your values keep you from sanctioning such a visit. Or, you wonder if it is fair to your daughter to say anything about the relationship. These are complicated issues, but in our experience it is important that you are honest with your son or daughter about where you are with your beliefs.

Hannah, a single mom, was faced with such a dilemma. Her 32-year-old daughter, Michelle, had recently shared with her that she was a lesbian and involved in a relationship with Susan. Michelle was bringing Susan to the family Christmas party and wanted to stay with Hannah while in town. Michelle being raised in a conservative Christian home knew her mother would not approve of the relationship. Hannah wanted to convey to Michelle that she loved and accepted her, but could not affirm her same-sex relationship. While listening to Michelle's concerns and honoring her ability to make her own choices, Hannah desired to be honest and explained to Michelle her views on same-sex behavior. She shared with Michelle that if her plans included bringing an opposite-sex partner home for a visit, the ground rules would be the same: any form of sexual immorality was not going to be allowed in her home. She invited them to stay if they were willing to abide by her guidelines. Michelle and Susan visited Hannah and were surprised by her love and acceptance of them, and admired her commitment to her values and beliefs.

Serve the Image of God in Your Son or Daughter

Consistent with listening and being honest, keep in mind that your son or daughter bears the image of God. This means several things to us, the first of which is that they deserve to be treated with respect. This means standing alongside your child as he or she wrestles with same-sex attraction. This means not belittling them or making fun of their choices, even if you disagree with them.

Serving the image of God in your son or daughter also means relating to them in ways that respect their choices but expresses concern for their well-being. This becomes clearer when we consider the alternatives. You do not serve the image of God in another by communicating to them that their life is their own and that you will support or condone whatever decisions they make. Of course, in one sense their life *is* their own and they *will* own their decisions; but from a Christian perspective, their life is forfeit to God, and God, through the work of the Holy Spirit, is active in the life of all Christians, setting them apart for His purposes.

Paul wanted his parents to "say anything." After disclosing to his mother and stepfather, Paul felt even more isolated by his family's reluctance to discuss his choices related to sexuality, dating, and marriage. For more than two years, no one in his family acknowledged his choice to engage in same-sex relationships. Paul's mother Anita, although she conveyed to Paul once that she did not agree with his "choice" to date someone of the same-sex, instead began to passively patronize Paul when he discussed his "friends." Not helping the situation was Paul's stepfather, who attempted to "lighten" the conversation by telling "gay jokes." Paul felt belittled by their actions and elicited the help of a counselor to provide him with strategies to communicate his needs to family members.

Be Realistic in Your Expectations

Some parents may expect too much, and some may have very few expectations for their children. With the recent ads from ex-gay ministries citing examples of people changing their sexual orientations, some parents may have the unrealistic expectations that their child can make a complete change in their sexual orientation. Sending this message to your child may set them up for feelings of failure and rejection, especially if they continue to invest time and financial and emotional resources in professional treatment or paraprofessional ministry to facilitate change. Even among those who are highly motivated to experience change, there are no easy answers or pat formulas to remove every vestige of same-sex attraction. Avoiding blaming your child and using "if only" statements, such as "If you would only do what they tell you, you would get better," "If you didn't hang around ____, you wouldn't have this problem," or "If you would only begin to wear makeup and fix yourself up."

Let's consider an example. Amanda, age 34, has struggled with same-sex attractions ever since she could remember. She dated rarely in high school and even less in college. Embracing the traditional Christian sexual ethic, Amanda refused to embrace herself as a lesbian and sought professional and paraprofessional help. Wanting her family's encouragement and support, Amanda decided to share her struggle with them. Various members of the family informed Amanda that they already knew she was "different," and as long as she was receiving help, that was all that mattered. For years, no one in Amanda's family overtly discussed her "situation;" they did however send her a number of subtle messages about her sexuality and, more importantly, her future. During a conversation with her father that centered around marriage and grandchildren, Amanda was surprised to hear her father's expectations for her. He commented, "I hope your brother and sister hurry up and get married because I want grandchildren before I am too old." When Amanda questioned the message he was sending, her father responded, "I never imagined with your problem that you would ever marry or have any children."

Although it is important to set realistic expectations for sons or daughters experiencing same-sex attractions, it is also essential that parents have some expectations. Balance is the key, and the preceding principles of listening, being honest, and serving the image of God in your child impact the discussions with your children around expectations.

Educate Yourself to Understand Your Child's Struggle

Picking up this book was a great start! And there are many other resources you can read to help you understand some of the most important issues related to same-sex attraction and behavior (see Appendix A). When you reflect on your child's struggle, it is important to recall that not every individual struggling with same-sex attraction is the same. Given that there are no pat formulas or easy answers, we encourage you to educate yourself about same-sex attraction, homosexual orientation, and what it means to integrate attractions into a "gay" identity. Talk with other parents. This may be easier through a local support group, but find out what types of resources are available for families and friends of individuals struggling with same-sex attraction (see Appendix B).

Your education is not merely academic. Be prepared to minister to your child when the opportunity arises. Now, we are not advocating that you send your child resources or lay a "coming out of homosexuality" book on your coffee table, these actions could close the door on communication, especially if your child has embraced a gay identity. Consider the parents in the next two scenarios, both wanted the best for their children, but had very different ways of displaying this.

Mary found out her son, Jacob, is living a gay lifestyle in California. Wanting to impact his community, Jacob became involved in a local gay committee. He informed his mother that he celebrates his sexuality and is not concerned by her disapproval of his lifestyle. Mary was beside herself and determined to find out every thing she could about homosexuality. Mary became an "expert." She read everything she could find on homosexuality and became involved in a parent's group for loved ones struggling with same-sex attraction. She planned on rescuing Jacob, from what—she was not sure. Mary began sending Jacob every newsletter, pamphlet, and book she could get her hands on. When Jacob would visit his mother, he was often faced with Scriptures strategically placed by his bedside and ex-gay literature on the coffee table. Mary meant no harm, and she only wanted what was best for her son. Sadly though, her efforts pushed Jacob away. Ending up in a counselor's office, Mary was encouraged to work through her own feelings about the choices that her son was making. Upon coming to terms with some of her fears, Mary was able to respond more lovingly to her son, instead of reacting to his choices.

Lois was a bit different than Mary when it came to responding to her child. Lois' daughter, Wendy, "came out" when she was in college. Although Lois had a similar reaction to Mary's, her plan to help Wendy was a bit different. Lois, not unlike Mary, read everything she could get her hands on. She began seeing a counselor and met with the director of a local ex-gay ministry. Lois was afforded timely advice early on that helped her respond to Wendy in a loving manner, respectful of her daughter's choices, yet uncompromising in her faith. One evening while Lois was preparing for bed, she received a call from Wendy. Distraught over a recent break up, Wendy poured her heart out to her mother. Through the conversation, Lois was able to understand her daughter's struggle more fully and respond to her needs due to her willingness to educate herself about the dynamics and issues involved in same-sex attraction. Toward the end of the conversation,

Wendy expressed her gratitude to her mother, by thanking her for her consistent loving response to her as a person, as her daughter. Wendy knew that her mother did not approve of her lifestyle, but she also knew how much her mother loved her.

It can be difficult to know how to respond to a son or daughter. The scenarios here are not meant to depict a "wrong" or "right" way of responding. What is probably more useful to you is to reflect on the ramifications of a variety of ways of responding to your child. What are the potential advantages of one response over another? What are the potential disadvantages?

It is also essential that you, as a parent, avail yourself of the resources in your local community, including your local church community, to help you provide your child with greater understanding and more practical support. This brings us to our last principle: prayer.

Commit Your Child to Prayer

Prayer reaches places that seem unreachable. Whether your child is open to discussing issues related to their sexuality, seeking help for unwanted same-sex attractions, not responsive to conversations about their sexuality, or extremely happy in a same-sex relationship, prayer knows no bounds. Parents often ask, "What can I do?" Prayer is at the top of the list. Some parents have responded with exasperation, "No, really, what can I do?" Prayer is not a second best response. It is as simple as whispering your child's name and as powerful as moving a mountain.

Carey, a young girl struggling with lesbianism once said, "It may not look like it right now, but divine love has and also will meet every human need." During sessions she spoke fondly of her aunt's great love for her and for her aunt's commitment to pray everyday for Carey's needs. Carey referred to it as "storming the gates of heaven," she remarked, "I believe my aunt has gone to places for me that angels fear to tread."

Siblings

Although the principles mentioned above for parents may also be applied to siblings, we wanted to mention some unique aspects of sibling relationships. Siblings of individuals experiencing same-sex attraction, in comparison to parents, are in a different and unique place of relationship. Unlike parents, siblings have a more pronounced horizontal relationship that brings with it a variety of issues that impact our lives. Some may be more likely to disclose their experiences with same-sex attraction and behavior to a sister or a brother. Siblings are in a unique position, as being a part of one another's "generation" or cohort, they may see some things similarly, and yet have the potential to offer a differing view.

Lynn has an older brother and a younger sister, and they all grew up in a tumultuous family environment. Each child was impacted by their environment and responded differently. During the time when Lynn met with her brother and sister to disclose her unwanted same-sex attractions, the siblings began to relate their own unique struggles to one another. Lynn and her siblings were afforded the opportunity to express their own unique issues, while hearing their sibling's perspectives. Lynn's disclosure opened doors of communication between her and her siblings; doors that she had yet to open with her parents.

Not all sibling interactions are supportive and encouraging. Just as siblings are in a unique position to offer words of healing and restoration, siblings can too respond in a manner that is destructive. The bond of siblinghood is powerful. As a brother or sister, you are in a position to offer a unique perspective for your sibling. We encourage you to prayerfully consider your responses to your loved one experiencing same-sex attractions.

Spouses

If you are a spouse of someone who experiences same-sex attraction, you too have unique concerns. In our experience spouses most typically are distressed because their spouse (a) thought their same-sex attraction was a "quirk" that would go away, (b) married for "treatment," or (c) thought they were "cured."

Individuals who Thought their Same-Sex Attraction was a "Quirk" that Would Go Away

The first experience is that of individuals who thought their same-sex attraction was a quirk that would go away. Rollo, age 38, presented in therapy shortly after his wife discovered that he had been downloading homosexual pornography through the Internet. Although he claims that he would have "eventually" sought therapy, his wife's discovery of the pornography was the catalyst. He stated that he is devoutly religious and a leader in his local community. He believes that same-sex behavior is immoral and that same-sex attractions are not God's intention for sexuality. During the sexual history,

Rollo stated that he and his wife are sexually active, and that when they are "emotionally connected" to one another, he has far less intense attractions to other men.

Rollo experienced same-sex attraction but thought it was something unusual, a quirk that he thought would go away over time. Once he was married and took on the responsibilities of being a husband, including engaging in a sexual relationship with his wife, he thought these experiences would disappear. Individuals like Rollo may or may not have disclosed their attractions to their wives, and they may minimize or deny the intensity of their attractions. Once such individuals are married, they often find themselves discouraged by ongoing experiences of same-sex attraction.

Individuals Who Married for "Treatment"

One particularly challenging concern is if your spouse married for "treatment." These individuals believe or have been counseled to believe that what they need is to marry—that the intimacy of marriage would untie any knots of sexual identity conflict that may exist: Ron,[1] age 32, had struggled with same-sex attraction since he was a teen. He had been in a few homosexual relationships, but had never fully identified as a gay man. Ron had never had a "successful" heterosexual relationship. A close friend and mentor told Ron that all he needed to do was meet a decent woman, get married, have kids, and his same-sex attractions would go away. Ron heeded his friend's advice, met a nice woman, got married, and immediately had a child. He has been married about two years, has an eighteen-month-old child, and presents in therapy as concerned and distressed over his ongoing attractions to men.

Oftentimes individuals who marry for treatment have been encouraged to do so by an influential person in their lives, such as a pastor or relative. They may have thought it best to pursue marriage as a way to extinguish their unwanted desires. Important issues that may come up have to do with your spouse's initial enthusiasm for this "treatment." Individuals often discuss their sustained resolve to work through their attractions and maintain their marriage. But you, as the spouse, may or may not know of your spouse's experiences or "treatment plan."

Individuals Who Thought They were "Cured"

Another experience is that of individuals who pursued professional or paraprofessional treatment and thought they were "cured" before they entered marriage. Often these persons present following several years of professional treatment or ministry involvement where they experienced a decrease in the intensity, frequency, or duration of same-sex attraction or behavior. Consider the following example. For as long as she has conscious memory, Cindy's preference has been for women. After making a personal commitment to Christianity in the fall of her senior year in college, Cindy sought out various treatments, both professional and paraprofessional, to cure her of her lesbianism. After two years, Cindy married and began attending an "ex-gay" ministry. She eventually became a small group leader for women in the ministry, sharing her story of change and healing from homosexuality. For three years, Cindy avoided any kind of physical intimacy with women, until she met and fell in love with a woman in the congregation of the church she attended. Cindy and her husband sought the help of a therapist to deal with the painful reality that she had not been cured.

Cindy's case illustrates the second presenting concern of individuals who entered marriage because they were told they were cured or genuinely believed themselves to be cured. They will often deny or minimize their level of attraction until it is brought out, and they are in crisis. Well-intentioned others may have set up unrealistic expectations that they will no longer have experiences with same-sex attraction. As a spouse, you may or may not know of the prior treatment your spouse was in, or of their "cure." Individuals may struggle with guilt and shame over their decision not to inform their partner, having thought, "Why should I tell them if I'm 'cured'? That's in the past." Common experience is the fear that their spouse would not have married them if they had known their past.

We are presenting a few common concerns faced by couples where one partner contends with same-sex attraction. However, it will be encouraging to know that some couples report being satisfied in their marriage, despite past and current struggles with one partner experiencing same-sex attraction. We refer to these couples as "resilient couples,"[2] couples where one partner experiences same-sex attraction but where they are reporting mutual satisfaction and do not experience themselves at risk for marital dissolution.

Although little research has been done in this area, we believe that there are several possible predictors of resilience. First, couples seem to do better if there is disclosure of the experiences of same-sex attraction, rather than discovery of same-sex attractions. In other words, it seems to be better if a husband tells his wife about his struggles than if his wife were to find an Internet history of her husband having visited dozens of gay pornography sites. While both disclosure and discovery can be threatening to a marriage's stability and a partner's sense of trust, discovery seems to call into question much more for a partner than an open, honest discussion of one partner's struggles.

Second, full disclosure seems better in most circumstances than partial disclosure. By "full" we do not mean that a spouse has to share every lustful thought or every experience of attraction or acting out behavior. What we mean is that sometimes a spouse will offer a partial disclosure by minimizing their experiences of same-sex attraction or framing the attractions as "in the past," when they are a very real and current struggle. These kinds of partial disclosures are essentially secrets, and secrets are difficult to keep in marriage, and they ultimately erode the sense of intimacy and trust that is so foundational to a close, supportive marriage partnership.

A third principle is that resilient couples tend to focus on their communication skills. They want to work on being clear with each other about what they are thinking and feeling, so that there are fewer misunderstandings that come from couples keeping to themselves and essentially feeling isolated from their partner.

Fourth, resilient couples tend to be open to accountability. Sometimes this happens in the marriage itself. Some spouses will do a monthly check of their computer's Internet history, just to function as an external source of accountability. Most couples find a small group or have the struggling spouse active in a small accountability group with members of the same sex where they can be honest about their daily experiences. These groups help the spouse who contends with same-sex attraction identity and resist the tendency to make excuses or rationalize ways of thinking or behaving that can compromise their life goals and what is in the best interest of their marriage.

We turn now to some of the key issues facing the church, the Body of Christ. Even if a person does not have a child or spouse who contends with same-sex attraction, we all have brothers and sisters in Christ who are courageously struggling to live faithfully before God in their present circumstances. So the next chapter is for all believers.

Reflections for Families

1. If you are a parent of a child who experiences same-sex attraction, what has made it particularly difficult to listen to your child's struggle with homosexuality? Are there times when you are afraid to be honest with your loved one? What is the relationship between listening and honesty in this difficult area?
2. What expectations, spoken or unspoken, do you have for your child? How might these expectations make it difficult for you to be a source of support? What can you do to work through your reactions and expectations, so that these are not a burden your child has to also bear at this time?
3. What have you done to educate yourself about the experiences your child is going through? Identify two or three specific advantages to you and to your relationship with your child of becoming more educated on the topic. What are some practical things you can do to learn more about your child's experience?
4. What does serving the image of God in your son or daughter mean to you? Take a few minutes to journal ten concrete and specific things you can do over the course of the next two to three weeks to serve the image of God in your child.
5. If your spouse experiences same-sex attraction, what have been some of the unique challenges you have faced in your marriage? In what ways do you encourage or support your spouse to address their issues?
6. If your sibling experiences same-sex attraction, what have been some of the unique challenges you have faced in your relationship? In what ways do you encourage or support your sibling to address their issues?

Chapter

9

A Word to the Church

> At present we are living "in between times," between the grace which we grasp by faith, and the glory which we anticipate in hope. Between them lies love. Yet love is generally what the Church has failed to show to homosexual people.[1]

In the preceding chapter we wrote about families because of the anguish so many parents and spouses report when loved ones struggle with same-sex attraction or behavior. These experiences can be devastating to families. But the broader church needs to be brought into this discussion. This is not an issue reserved just for those families where a loved one experiences same-sex attraction or engages in same-sex behavior. From a Christian perspective, we have a responsibility to one another and to these families, so that we are not letting them struggle in isolation, ashamed to discuss these problems honestly with fellow Christians who participate in the same redemptions and sanctification.

But how has our church become a place where these concerns are kept secret? Certainly there are those in the church who are trying to change the Christian sexual ethic, to say that same-sex behavior is not immoral, that the church should sanction same-sex unions and ordain ministers who engage in same-sex behavior. But that is not what we are talking about. We are talking about what makes the church a place where people are *unable* to struggle with any number of concerns, same-sex attraction and behavior being among them.

What often happens in the local Christian community is that individuals who struggle with same-sex attraction live in isolation from others. Churches often rank order moral concerns and the church community can send messages about which sins are more tolerable for community life. For example, as we mentioned in Chapter 2, it is generally acceptable in most conservative churches to admit to certain struggles, such as pride or envy. But it is much more difficult to have an open and honest struggle with homosexuality. This makes it very difficult for the person who struggles with homosexuality to find much needed support. Homosexuality is definitely a taboo topic in most churches today.

What happens if a person shares their struggles in a church community that is not mature enough to respond pastorally to these experiences? A young man Mark knew several years ago had been diagnosed with AIDS. He entered counseling wanting to fight the virus and was fully confident that God intended to heal him. In the end he did die of an opportunistic infection as a result of the depletion of his immune system. In the course of our meetings and preparation for his death, he shared that his pastor learned that the young man contracted HIV through homosexual sex. The pastor insisted that the young man confess his sin of homosexuality before the entire congregation. After some consideration the young man decided to obey his pastor. This was his Christian community, it was his lifeline in his life in Christ, and he had no other place to turn for fellowship. This was a very painful experience for this young man. He was so ashamed to speak publicly of his homosexual relationship, and he was struggling to maintain his own sense of self in the face of his terminal illness.

The pastor called him a week or so after his public confession and informed him that he had not disclosed enough information to have fulfilled his responsibilities to the community. He was informed that he had to make a second, more detailed public confession or face church discipline. Again, the young man considered this request and we discussed the potential devastating effects of following through on such a request. But the young man felt he had no other options. It was his family church. It was his home in Christ. He agreed to share a more detailed public confession before the entire congregation and so fulfill his responsibilities to the community of faith as understood by his pastor.

This story is startling for many reasons. Not the least of these is that it reminds us of how powerful religious communities and religious leaders are in our lives. Christians grow in their faith communities. Ideally, a Christian finds a church home where they are nurtured in their faith, challenged to grow in areas where God is at work in their lives, and afforded the opportunity to participate in corporate confession and worship. Churches have the potential to be an incredible healing resource to broken people. But they also have the potential of being of great damage to a person who is at a vulnerable place in their lives. Again, there are no easy answers, but we want to share with you a few principles and then illustrate the application of these principles through various examples. Some of these principles will be similar to those offered to families, but applied differently.

Principles for the Body of Christ

Listen as a Follower of Christ

It is important to listen in the way a follower of Christ should listen to others. People have been preached at and have heard things from religious leaders and followers, and they are often prepared for the worst. So much of listening, in fact, is often making up for past abuses by steering clear of clichés and quick fixes.

Share the Truth as a Follower of Christ

Just as people benefit when Christians listen to them as followers of Christ, so too people benefit from hearing the truth spoken by followers of Christ in a way that honors Christ's name. Often it is not *what* is said that offends people, but *how* it is said. It is difficult for people to believe that you love them and care about their well-being if you are shouting at them from a picket line. But this is an extreme example. It is difficult for people to believe you love them if you only say it but are not a loving presence in their life. Before you share your perspective on sexuality and sexual ethics, have you earned the right to be heard? What would that mean in the present relationship?

An illustration of this can be found in Mel White's book, *Stranger at the Gate*. Mel shares his struggles with homosexuality and ultimately his decision to leave his wife and children and pursue a same-sex relationship. He shares the negative reactions he received from many Christians, including several prominent Christian leaders. The most impressive Christian presence in that book, in our opinion, is Phillip Yancey, who is a well-known Christian writer and long-time friend of Mel White. Yancey disagreed with Mel's decisions and did not condone Mel's behavior, but there was no question of his love for his friend. This is the kind of sustained presence that Christians should strive to emulate. Speak the truth but only after earning the right to be heard, and only out of the context of a relationship where mutual regard, respect, and love is clearly evidenced.

Serve the Image of God in the Individual

As we mentioned earlier, the phrase "what would Jesus do?" is less helpful than the phrase, "how did Jesus live?" He lived in close proximity to those who needed grace the most. He became a part of their lives, and in His service to them, He modeled a higher calling for responding to the needs of others.

Maggie works at a local hospice for AIDS patients. Every Saturday, for one year, she takes the bus downtown to a section of the city that few people in her church know exists. Maggie is a 72-year-old widower. Her husband died three years ago, and since that time her adult children have been encouraging Maggie to get out and enjoy the services in her community. Maggie met David at a bingo game. David, a member of the youth group, was there to help the senior citizens and provide them with refreshments. Striking up a relationship, David began to confide in Maggie about his same-sex attractions and behaviors. Believing he could trust her, David told Maggie that he had AIDS. Although most of this was foreign to Maggie, she loved David as modeled by Christ's love for her. During the last months of his life, Maggie stayed by David's side, reading to him, singing songs for him, and helping when she could in his daily care.

Respond to the Person and Not the Behavior

Randy stood on the side of the road where a number of anti-gay demonstrators had assembled. There was a gay parade in town and he wanted to make sure his voice was heard among the many. Randy felt that it was his duty to proclaim the gospel to homosexuals. The sign Randy held stated, "Gays will go to hell!" A Scripture passage was scribbled below this statement. Randy screamed Scriptures and proclamations of God's wrath for over two hours. Following the parade he went to a local restaurant with a number of his church friends. While walking out of the restaurant, Randy tripped down some steps. At the bottom of the steps, a young man reached for his hand, helped him to his feet, brushed him off, and made sure he was all right. As Randy thanked him, the young said, "You don't remember me? I was in the parade today, and you said I was a sinner going to hell." Once Randy returned home, he sat on the sofa and tried to remember any of the faces that passed by his place on the parade route. Randy could not remember one.

Not everyone in the church is like Randy. Believe it or not, Randy was sure he was doing right in the sight of God. Individuals struggling with same-sex attractions and behaviors are people, created in the image of God. They are not their sexuality, anymore than they are their jobs, cars, or hobbies. We can communicate with people, but it is impossible to communicate with a behavior. Acceptance of a person is not synonymous with approval of their behavior. Again, we must ask ourselves, "How did Jesus live?"

Embrace Truth over Stereotypes and Labels

The greatest barrier to love is fear. The Bible assures us that perfect love casts out fear. Many in the church have struggled with a variety of fears related to homosexuals and lesbians. "Will they be attracted to me?" "Will they 'come on' to me?" "Will my children be safe around them?" What if someone sees me with ____ and thinks I'm a lesbian?" Stereotypes and labels promote a distorted view of individuals struggling with same-sex attractions, but more importantly it sends a message to the individual that they are different and undesirable. Terms such as fag, sissy, dike, and queer have been used to belittle and demoralize.

Hoping to help Janice build connections in her local church, Lori encouraged her to join a cell group. Janice wanted little to do with the church. She was a pastor's daughter and had, according to her, paid her dues in the den of hypocrisy. With great hesitation, Janice began attending a cell group on Friday nights. Jane, another member of the cell group, joked frequently in her circle of friends that she could spot a "lesbo" a mile away. Little did she know that Janice secretly struggled with same-sex attraction. Janice entered counseling swearing that she would never return to the group. She was encouraged to focus on the members of the group who acted in a mature and loving manner, versus focusing all of her attention. Despite her hesitation, Janice remained in the cell group, building a number of strong, safe relationships.

A similar concern is the tendency among local churches to relate to men and women based on stereotypes. The church sometimes confuses contemporary Western stereotypes of men and women with biblical understandings of what it means to be a man or a woman. This can range from assumptions about what men and women like to do, to parenting behaviors, or hobbies. The stereotypes themselves can limit what a specific man or woman feels they can do so that their activities qualify as sufficiently masculine or feminine. There is no need for the church to make a difficult situation worse by treating Western stereotypes as biblical.

Act in a Manner that is Consistent with the Virtues of Faith, Hope, and Love

Individuals who struggle with same-sex attractions are not beyond hope. Yes, addressing unwanted same-sex desires takes a great deal of effort and may involve uncomfortable levels of stress and frustration. However, just like there is hope for overcoming any signature sin, there is hope for strugglers of unwanted same-sex attractions.

We, as the body of Christ, must tangibly demonstrate our faith in God—that He is working in the lives of individuals who struggle with same-sex attractions. Relating in an attitude of love, while ministering hope, speaks volumes to these individuals. We as a church must be willing to communicate to individuals, whatever sin they may be struggling with, that they are not isolated in their struggle, that they are not beyond hope, and that they are not cursed and condemned by others. All have fallen short of the glory of God.

What are tangible ways in which the church can minister to individuals struggling with same-sex attractions? The church can begin by educating their parishioners, replacing stereotypes and labels with the truth. Network with a local paraprofessional ministry to people struggling with same-sex attraction or any number of sexual concerns. Perhaps the local ministry is struggling to develop and find ways to best serve the local community. Your church might provide support and also oversight, so that there is more accountability among the leadership and those providing ministry to those in need. If there is no such group in your area, pray about offering a support group through your church. Be willing to establish safe and established accountability partners for individuals who seek spiritual direction and growth.

Casting a Vision

We want to close this chapter by casting a vision of a church that ministers effectively to people with all kinds of struggles, including sexual struggles. Among these sexual struggles, some will struggle with same-sex attraction and behavior. Here is our best description:

Pastoral Vision, Transparency, and Integrity

Pastoral vision. The church we envision has a pastor with a vision for ministry to the broken. This ministry presupposes that everyone in the congregation struggles with something. Everyone in the congregation has a cluster of signature struggles that are unique to them, and the pastor "sees" this as a premise for ministry to all who participate in the life of the church. But the vision is not just a vision of the need; it is a vision for the ministry. Pastoral vision begins to see the local community of faith as a source of mutual aid and support. Perhaps you have heard of the large statue of Jesus on the cross in Europe on which Jesus has lost his hands. Under it is a note that reads, "Jesus has only our hands to do His work." The pastor has seen this cross and believes that God ministers to people through people, and the local community of faith is the place to begin.

Pastoral transparency. The pastor shares personal struggles with the cluster of signature struggles that are a part of the pastor's life. The pastor need not be an "ex-gay" or a former sex addict. But the pastor shares the humanity of the struggle—this is something everyone in the congregation can identify with.

Pastoral integrity. The pastor would be a person of integrity. This means living out with some consistency what is said publicly. The vision works itself out in practical ways only to the extent that the leadership in the church practices what they preach. Calls for support and charitable giving can be heard because the pastor is the first to offer support and give gifts to others. The pastor can speak to accountability groups because the pastor is active in a small group with others.

Congregational Interdependence and Humility

Congregational interdependence. In response to the pastoral vision, integrity, and transparency, the congregation acts on what they hear and see. Their responsiveness takes the burden of the vision off of the pastor and places it onto the backs of the parishioners. They are responsive to one another because they recognize their inherent interdependence on one another. They need each other to make it, because God gives them each other as expressions of His love and longstanding presence.

At a practical level, volunteers from the congregation coordinate small group training and a gathering of resources. They set up workshops and consultations to address any number of concerns facing specific individuals. There will also be those in the congregation with special expertise in a wide variety of fields, including medicine, mental health, community access to resources, and education. These members make themselves available as direct resources or indirect resources insofar as they function as gatekeepers to various community resources.

In this congregation the people themselves are seen as resources. As people make strides in their own areas of struggle, they become resources to others. So there is a cycling of resources that takes place. Every learner becomes a teacher; every teacher still learns because the atmosphere fosters a kind of "life-long learning" in all areas of spiritual growth and maturity.

Congregational humility. People in the congregation also provide resources out of a spirit of humility. There is no one-upmanship in what is offered or what is needed. Needs and wants are addressed for all who need them because the congregation recognizes their shared standing in need of the grace and mercy they receive daily from God. The interdependence and cycling of resources leads to this, because people realize they need God, and so they need each other, because God uses people to extend His love, grace, and mercy.

Reflections for the Church

1. Listening and truth telling can be two important but very difficult principles to follow and hold in tension. How would someone who struggles with same-sex attraction describe your listening skills? Would someone say of you that the way you listen marks you as a follower of Christ? Why or why not?
2. What have you found are the keys to telling people the truth while avoiding a personal attack that may drive a wedge between you and another person? Do you know others who seem to keep this in balance? Describe what you like about the way they relate to others. What would it look like for you to practice some of these skills?
3. Ask God to guide you into relationships with people who struggle with same-sex attraction, and ask God to give you the ears to listen and the words to share, as well as the wisdom and discernment to know when to listen and when to share the truth.
4. Have there been times when you have believed and acted upon stereotypes and labels? How has this gotten in the way of the kind of person you want to be in your relationships with others? When have you successfully avoided stereotypes and labels?
5. What does it mean to you to act in a manner that is consistent with the virtues of faith, hope, and love? What are tangible ways in which you can minister faith, hope, and love to individuals struggling with same-sex attractions?

6. In what ways do you see your church responding to the needs of individuals struggling with same-sex attraction? What are two or three practical things you can do to help your church consider support for a local ministry or to develop its own outreach and support to people who struggle with same-sex attraction?

Chapter

10

A Final Word to Strugglers

> Finally, Brothers, goodbye. Aim for perfection, listen to my appeal, be of one mind, live in peace. And the God of love and peace will be with you. May the grace of the Lord Jesus Christ, and the love of God, and the fellowship of the Holy Spirit be with you all. (2 Corinthians 13:11, 14)

To say that struggling with unwanted same-sex attraction is difficult is an understatement. Many of you have had to face, whether directly or indirectly, the stereotypes and stigma associated with this signature struggle. We hope the material in this book will help you as you continue to walk out your salvation and live faithfully before the Lord.

We would like to offer you a few practical suggestions as you continue on your life's journey. We think of this as consolidating the gains you have made in the work you are doing on your sexual identity. This includes thinking through practical strategies for preventing relapse. We will then close this chapter and this book by offering you a few principles to keep in mind as you relate with family, friends, and your local church community.

Consolidating Gains

As you begin to achieve and maintain the freedom to choose chastity in your intimate relationships, you may wonder at what point you have been successful in reaching your life goals. Although there is no set "end point" you reach (recall that this is a *process* not a *program*), you might review what you have set out for yourself as goals in the area of intimacy, sexual behavior, and sexual identity.

Here are a few things you might consider:

1. Can you achieve and maintain chastity?
2. Do you know the situations that are homosexually stimulating to you?
3. Do you experience less frequent and less intense experiences of same-sex attraction?
4. Can you recognize the relationships among physical sensations, thoughts, feelings, and behavior?
5. Are you getting your emotional needs met through close, nonsexual relationships with members of the same and opposite sex?
6. Do you recognize your patterns of disconnecting and reconnecting with others and consistently choose self-soothing behaviors that are consistent with your goals?
7. Can you correctly and consistently identify the "parts" of yourself and can you have your "self" take a lead in responsible decision-making?
8. Do you regularly ask yourself "constraint questions," and can you identify and remove constraints?
9. Do you have a firm sense of your self-identity that is consistent with your life goals?
10. Do you recognize your unique areas of struggle and how God is at work setting you apart for His purpose?

Anticipating Challenges

In addition to honestly answering the questions above, you might take a moment to identify the top three most difficult challenges you think you will face in your ability to maintain the strides you have made following our approach. These challenges may include seeing old friends, hearing hateful stories about "gays" at church, seeing others in dating relationships, or any number of specific challenges.

You can then begin to identify what might keep you from responding to those challenges in ways that are consistent with your life goals. Again, these are constraints. What are the possible constraints that may be especially challenging to you? How could those constraints be removed? Completing Worksheet 10.1 will help you think through some of the specific challenges you may face and what changes may need to be made in anticipation of difficult circumstances. Begin by identifying three things that you believe will present as real challenges to your ability to maintain progress. Then reflect on what might keep you from addressing these challenges. List three or so things that might be a concern, and then reflect on what you have written down. Identify the constraint or constraints that may keep you from addressing your challenges, and then identify three or more concrete and specific strategies for removing the constraints. This worksheet can be used as you make gains and to help you prepare for the challenge of maintaining strides. Remember that for most people there is no substitute for good planning and foresight.

Identifying Signature Patterns of Relapse

Everyone who struggles with their experiences of same-sex attraction and works through our approach will have their own unique pattern of potential relapse. What do we mean by relapse? Think about Mike, a young man who was born with a propensity to alcoholism. There is no one "cause" of alcoholism, but Mike does struggle in this area and has followed a 12-step program at AA (a few times) on his road to recovery. As a recovering alcoholic, Mike has not used alcohol for over 12 months, but he still occasionally experiences cravings for alcohol. After all, he liked drinking, and he enjoyed the social relationships associated with his patterns of drinking. At what point should Mike consider himself to have experienced "success" in his treatment? Is it following the last time he took a drink? Is it if he abstains for two years? Does the fact that he experiences cravings mean that he has failed, even if he were never to drink again? What happens if Mike were to experience a relapse?

What is particularly interesting about this comparison is that, in AA, participants are always encouraged to think of themselves as vulnerable to relapse. They are told about the "abstinence-violation" effect, that is, the experience people have where if they have a drink (thereby violating their commitment to abstinence from alcohol) they feel they have "blown it," and they go on a drinking binge. This can be incredibly destructive to a person's attempts to change the way they live as someone vulnerable to alcohol misuse.

When people who experience same-sex attraction choose to work toward chastity and related goals, they face a similar challenge in how they think of what constitutes "success." They could think of success quite narrowly as being rid of every vestige of same-sex attraction. However, as we have already discussed, this is unlikely for most people who contend with same-sex attraction. And it is quite a strict standard when compared to the standards established in AA and other programs. What are the alternatives? People could define success as living faithfully before God. This could include being honest with God about experiencing same-sex attraction. This could mean putting in place strategies to help maintain chastity in relation to one's behaviors and thought life. This could mean accepting God's grace when one struggles more with same-sex thoughts or fantasies, or even when one relapses through same-sex behavior. So success can be defined quite broadly but very much in keeping with how success is defined in AA and other programs. But along with a broad definition of success, comes a vigilance that one is always at risk. What you would not want to do is define yourself by your struggle (though in AA you would tend to think of yourself as always an alcoholic). In this approach, while you might always end up thinking of yourself as a person who experiences same-sex attraction, you need not define yourself by your struggles, as there are so many other aspects of yourself you can identify with, including your identity as a religious person ("I am a Christian," or "I am a Jew,") or your identity based on your gender ("I am a male," or "I am a female.")

To return to the question of relapse, we would encourage you to identify your "signature" patterns of relapse, as no two are identical, and you can really benefit from learning more about your own. Use Worksheet 10.2 to help you make a plan that specifically addresses your signature patterns. You might begin by thinking clearly about your goals. For example, if chastity in thoughts or behavior is your goal, then it is rather clear what you are striving for.

The second step is to identify what are referred to as Seemingly Unimportant Decisions or SUDs. These are the countless day-to-day decisions that seem reasonable at the time, but which actually place you in a position (physically or emotionally) to relapse. These may go back to specific items, places, or relationships that we discussed earlier, or they may point to daily routines that are fine for now, but over time these weekly or monthly patterns of behavior may make you vulnerable to relapse.

Third, when you make seemingly unimportant decisions, you place yourself in "at-risk" situations. You may put yourself at risk because you now have a greater likelihood of thinking, fantasizing, or behaving in ways that are contrary to your goals.

The fourth step is a lapse in either thought or behavior that falls short of a relapse. For example, spending time alone with someone you find attractive might be viewed as an at-risk situation, while giving each other backrubs may be a behavior that comes close to, but falls short of, a relapse.

There is a key moment that follows a lapse that either leads to (a) a correction, or (b) giving up to the thought, fantasy, or behavior. Often the giving up is fueled by self-statements, such as "I've already gone too far by giving this backrub. I've crossed the line. I may as well do it." You are essentially saying that you have gone too far to put on the brakes, and you may as well give up on trying.

The final step in a pattern of relapse is the actual relapse. For the person who has had chastity as his or her goal, this is actively engaging in same-sex fantasy or behavior.

Then use Worksheet 10.3 to begin to put a plan in place that serves as an "Alternative to Relapse." This is a good worksheet to use as you begin to make strides in your life goals. Just as you are feeling you are getting the hang of this approach and you feel you are making progress, it is time for you to set up a plan for how you would respond to a potential relapse. You are essentially making a plan for some of the most difficult circumstances you may face, and you are identifying in advance the concrete and practical steps you can take so that you live your life consistent with the beliefs and values you hold about same-sex attraction and behavior. Begin to see each step in the "Alternative to Relapse" plan as a key decision point, and ask your accountability partner or support group to process this with you and be available to you when you most need their help and support.

Begin by clearly identifying your goals. If chastity in thoughts or behavior is your goal, then write this down. Then identify alternatives to the seemingly unimportant decisions you wrote down in Worksheet 10.2. If you found yourself having made a seemingly unimportant decision, what can you actually do as an alternative in that moment? Remember, these are the kinds of decisions that place you in an "at-risk" situation. What can you do if you find yourself in an at-risk situation? Do you have 24-hour access to a supportive friend and accountability partner? How will you respond if you have a lapse in thinking or behavior? If you have a lapse in behavior, it is important that your thoughts resist the tendency to "go for it" once you've crossed a line. This is a natural human reaction, but it is one that can also be resisted if you remind yourself that you have experienced a lapse, but that that does not have to mean you follow through on it. You can stop and contact your support system and continue to work toward your life goals.

We turn now to a few closing words of encouragement. What follows are key principles for you to consider as you relate to family, friends, and your local church community.

Closing Principles

Be patient, not everyone is going to reject you. Rejection—this simple word brings up a plethora of images and emotions. We have all felt the sting of rejection and have reacted in various ways. Some of us build walls, close people off, others move on to new relationships, hoping to find acceptance. Unfortunately, you will be rejected. Unfortunately, the church has responded inappropriately at times to individuals struggling with various difficulties, so have we, and so have you. This might be a cup difficult to drink from. All have fallen short. No one is exempt. With that said, we want to encourage you to put aside some of your expectations of rejection and lay a hold of patience. In a spirit of love and humility, let us look for the good in our family and churches, encouraging one another to live faithfully before Christ.

Educate, become a part of the solution. In the spirit of St. Augustine, where there is ignorance, sow lots of patience and knowledge. Who would better know your struggle than you would, and who would be better to share yourself to others than you would? Now, we are not advocating that everyone who reads this book should become a spokesperson for individuals struggling with unwanted same-sex attraction. Going about telling everyone of your struggle is probably not a wise choice, but there are other ways to become part of the solution. Where you are in the model of sexual identity development and synthesis may also help determine what you feel you can do to be a part of the solution. Those who are further along in reaching and maintaining their life goals may want to provide the church library or the pastors with materials that may be helpful. If you are an individual who is comfortable disclosing in your local church community, leading a small group discussion where stereotypes and misconceptions are addressed may help facilitate open and honest communication between parishioners. Remember, not everyone is going to be accepting; however, not everyone is going to be rejecting. When both parties turn from one another, the gap between them can only get bigger, but once someone turns and is willing to remain in relationship, solutions to the problems that exist are possible.

Know when to share your struggle with others. When do you share your struggle with others? All of us, regardless of our signature struggles are faced with answering this question. Cloud and Townsend, in their book *Safe People, Safe Places*, offer a number of principles for individuals hoping to connect safely with others. This book is a great resource for anyone desiring to make healthy connections with others, while maintaining safe and appropriate boundaries. Not everyone is in a place to respond appropriately to your struggle, and we encourage you to prayerfully consider your choices to disclose to family, friends, and individuals within your church community.

Submit yourself to accountability. There is no such thing as a "lone ranger Christian." We are not meant to walk this earthly journey alone. We were created for fellowship and relationship. As the Body of Christ, we celebrate our victories together and grieve our losses together. A body is just that, an interrelated system of parts acting in one accord. The problem comes when the feet want to go in one direction and the head in another. What would happen if your toes all decided to go their own way without consulting with the rest of your body? Chaos, and your body wouldn't get very far. Accountability is not meant to control or manipulate, accountability is a gift and an integral aspect of the sanctification process. A support group is one possible resource for support and accountability. We mentioned Exodus International, Homosexuals Anonymous, and Courage as three of a variety of Christian support groups. We encourage you to consider such a group (see Appendix B). As with the process of iron sharpening iron, accountability calls forth the image and character of Christ within us.

Reflections on A Final Word to Strugglers:

1. Read again from the list of questions we raised as we wrote about consolidating gains. As you read, what specific things will have changed in your life that will clearly indicate that you have made gains in reaching your life goals? In other words, how will you know that you have made strides as you continue to live your life following this new trajectory?
2. What does the term 'accountability' mean for you? What responsibility do you have to others in the Body of Christ? Think of two or three ways in which you can encourage accountability in your circle of friends and local church community.
3. When do you find it difficult to be patient with others? In what ways could you promote a spirit of love and patience within your family, your circle of friends, and your local church community?
4. Depending upon where you are in your experience of reaching and maintaining your life goals, how do you see yourself becoming part of the solution? Write down two or three ways in which you can impact your local church community. What would it be like for you to educate your family or friends about your struggle with same-sex attractions?
5. What have been your experiences sharing your struggle with others? How have you reacted to the struggle of others? When would you feel safe sharing your struggles with others? What do you think are the potential benefits and drawbacks of participating in a support and accountability group with others who can share their experiences with similar struggles?

Worksheet 10.1. Anticipating Challenges

What three things do you anticipate will challenge your ability to maintain progress?

1. ____

____

2. ____

____

3. ____

____

What might keep you from addressing these challenges?

1. ____

____

2. ____

____

3. ____

____

Identify constraint(s):____

Identify strategies that would help you overcome these constraints:

1. ____

____

2. ____

____

3. ____

____

Worksheet 10.2. Pattern of Relapse

Directions: (1) Write down your treatment goal, (2) List Seemingly Unimportant Decision, (3) Describe at-risk situation, (4) Identify lapse in thinking or behavior, and (5) Describe relapse.

Pattern	Description
Chastity (or other treatment goal)	
Seemingly Unimportant Decision	
At-Risk-Situation	
Lapse in Thinking or Behavior	
Relapse	

Worksheet 10.3. Alternatives to Relapse

Directions: (1) Write down your treatment goal, (2) Identify alternatives to the Seemingly Unimportant Decision, (3) List alternatives when in that at-risk situation, (4) Identify what you could do if you had a lapse in thinking or behavior, and (5) Specify alternative to relapse.

Pattern	Description
Chastity (or other treatment goal)	
Seemingly Unimportant Decision	
At-Risk-Situation	
Lapse in Thinking or Behavior	
Relapse	

Appendix

A

Selected Reading Resources on Homosexuality & Sexual Identity

Balch, D. (Ed.) (2000). *Homosexuality, science, and the "plain sense" of scripture*. Grand Rapids, MI: Eerdmans.
Divergent views on ethics, Scripture, and science

Bergner, M. (1995). *Setting love in order*. Grand Rapids, MI: Baker
Healing ministry/evangelical

Comiskey, A. (1989). *Pursuing sexual wholeness*. Lake Mary, FL: Creation House.
Healing ministry/evangelical

Consiglio, W. (1991). *Homosexual no more*. Wheaton, IL: Victor.
Healing ministry/evangelical

Dallas, J. (1991). *Desires in conflict*. Harvest House.
Healing ministry/evangelical

Davies, R., & Rentzel, L. (1994). *Coming out of homosexuality*. Downers Grove, IL: InterVarsity Press.
Evangelical

Gagnon, R. (2002). *The Bible and homosexual practice*. Lexington, KY: Abingdon.
Theological/analysis

Harvey, J. (1996). *The truth about homosexuality: The cry of the faithful*. San Francisco: Ignatius.
Catholic

Harvey, J. (1996). *The homosexual person: New directions in pastoral care*. San Francisco: Ignatius.
Catholic

Jones, S., & Yarhouse, M. (2000). *Homosexuality: The use of scientific research in the church's moral debate*. Downers Grove, IL: InterVarsity Press.
Theoretical/scientific/evangelical

Moberly, E. (1983). *Homosexuality: A new Christian ethic*. Greenwood, South Carolina: The Attic Press.
Theoretical

Nicolosi, J. (1993). *Healing homosexuality: Case stories of reparative therapy*. New York: Jason Aronson.
Professional/clinical case examples

Nicolosi, J. (1993). *Reparative therapy of male homosexuality*. New York: Jason Aronson.
Professional audience/reparative therapy

Payne, L. (1981). *The broken image*. Wheaton, IL: Crossway Books.
Healing ministry/evangelical

Prichard, R. (1992). *A wholesome example: Sexual morality and the Episcopal Church*. Lexington, KY: Bristol Books.
Theological/ecclesiastical analysis

Satinover, J. (1996). *Homosexuality and the politics of truth*. Grand Rapids, MI: Baker.
Theoretical/evangelical

Schmidt, T. (1994) *Straight and narrow? Compassion and clarity in the homosexuality debate*. Downers Grove, IL: InterVarsity.
Theoretical/evangelical

Siegel, E. (1988). *Female homosexuality: Choice without volition.* Hillsdale, NJ: The Analytic Press.
Professional audience

Siker, J. (Ed.) (1994). *Homosexuality in the church: Both sides of the debate.* Louisville, KY: Westminstry John Knox Press.
Divergent views on ethics, Scripture, and science

Webb, W. J. (2001). *Slaves, women and homosexuals: Exploring the hermeneutics of cultural analysis.* Downers Grove, IL: InterVarsity.
Theological/analysis

Wold, D. J. (1998). *Out of order: Homosexuality in the Bible and Ancient Near East.* Grand Rapids, MI: Baker.
Theological/analysis

Worthen, A., & Davies, B. (1996). *Someone I love is gay: How family and friends can respond.* Downers Grove, IL: InterVarsity Press.
Evangelical/family resource

Yamamoto, J. (Ed.). (1990). *The crisis of homosexuality.* Wheaton, IL: Victor Books.
Evangelical

Yarhouse, M., & Jones, S. (1997). The homosexual client. In R. K. Sanders (Ed.), *Christian counseling ethics.* Downers Grove, IL: InterVarsity Press.
Ethics/counseling issues

Yarhouse, M. (2001). *Expanding alternatives to same-sex attraction and behavior: Clinical modules for informed consent, assessment, and intervention.* Self-published, Virginia Beach, Virginia.
Professional audience, clinical workbook

Appendix

B

Selected Religion-Based Ministries

Umbrella Organizations:

Exodus International North America
P.O. Box 77652
Seattle, WA 98177-0652
Phone: (206) 784-7799
Internet: www.exodusinternational.org

Homosexuals Anonymous Fellowship Services
P.O. Box 7881
Reading, PA 19603
Phone: (610) 376-1146
Internet: http://members.aol.com/hawebpage

Courage (Roman Catholic)
c/o St. John the Baptist Church
210 West 31st Street
New York, NY 10001
Phone: (212) 268-1010
Email: NYCourage@aol.com
HTTP://courageRC.org

Independent Christian Ministries:

International Healing Foundations, Inc.
P.O. Box 901
Bowie, MD 20718-0901
Phone: (301) 805-6111
Email: IHF90@aol.com

Isaiah 56 Ministries
Isaiah Christian Church
2703 N. Fitzhugh
Dallas, TX 75204
Phone: (214) 823-9893
Email: twier@isaiah.org
Internet: http://www.isaiah.org/

McLean Ministries
P.O. Box 98 DTS
Boone, NC 28607
Phone: (828) 297-1877

Pastoral Care Ministries
Leanne Payne
P.O. Box 1313
Wheaton, IL 60189
Phone: (630) 510-0487

Redeemed Life
Mario Bergner
Church of the Resurrection
1825 College Avenue, Ste. 160
Wheaton, IL 60187
Phone: (630) 668-0661

RENEW
Christopher Austin, Ph.D.
P.O. Box 153429
Irving, Texas 75015-3429
Phone: (972) 986-0150
Email: renew@flash.net
Internet: www.flash.net/~renew

Jewish

Jews Offering New Alternatives to Homosexuality (JONAH)
PO Box 313
Jersey City, NJ 07303
Phone: (202) 433-3444

Latter Day Saints (Mormon)

Evergreen International
211 East 300 South, Suite 206
Salt Lake City, Utah 84111
Phone: 1-800-391-1000
Internet: www.evergreen-intl.org

Endnotes

Chapter 1: Sexual Identity

1. This definition is in keeping with Stanley E. Althof's definition as cited in his chapter, "Erectile Dysfunction: Psychotherapy with Men and Couples," in S. R. Leiblum, & R. C. Rosen (Eds.), *Principles and Practices of Sex Therapy* (3rd edition) (New York: Guilford, 2000), pp. 242-275.
2. See, for example, Mario Bergner, *Setting Love in Order* (Grand Rapids, MI: Baker, 1995); Andrew Comiskey, *Pursuing Sexual Wholeness* (Lake Mary, FL: Creation House,1989); William Consiglio, *Homosexual No More* (Wheaton, IL: Victor, 1991); and Robert Davies and Lori Rentzel, *Coming Out of Homosexuality* (Downers Grove, IL: InterVarsity Press, 1993).
3. See Chapter 5 from Stanton L. Jones and Mark A. Yarhouse, *Homosexuality: The Use of Scientific Research in the Church's Moral Debate* (Downers Grove, IL: InterVarsity Press, 2000).
4. Kim W. Schaeffer, R. A. Hyde, T. Kroencke, B. McCormick, & L. Nottebaum, "Religiously-Motivated Sexual Orientation Change," *Journal of Psychology and Christianity*, 2000, Vol. 19, No. 1, pp. 61-70; Kim W. Schaeffer, Lynn Nottebaum, P. Smith, K. Dech, & J. Krawczyk, "Religiously-Motivated Sexual Orientation Change: A Follow-Up Study," *Journal of Psychology and Theology*, 1999, Vol. 27, pp. 329-337.
5. Robert L. Spitzer, "Two Hundred Subjects Who Claim to have Changed their Sexual Orientation from Homosexual to Heterosexual." In Phillip A. Bialer (Chair), *Clinical Issues and Ethical Concerns Regarding Attempts to Change Sexual Orientation: An Update.* Paper presented at the annual meeting of the American Psychiatric Association, New Orleans, Louisiana, May 9, 2001.
6. Mark A. Yarhouse, "Sexual Identity Development: The Influence of Valuative Frameworks on Sexual Identity Synthesis," *Psychotherapy*, 2001, Vol. 38, No. 3, pp. 331-341. The discussion that follows is based upon this model and adapted from the article, Mark A. Yarhouse, "Reorientation or Identity Synthesis? Meta-

physical Reflections on the Current Ethical Debate," *Christian Bioethics* (in press).

7. There have been many theories as to the origins of same-sex attraction, including the theory that biology contributes significantly to one's experiences of same-sex attraction. Other theories include various factors from one's environment. For example, some professionals believe that difficulties in parent-child relationships contribute to a person's experiences of same-sex attraction. Most professionals today, however, acknowledge an "interactionist hypothesis" for the origins of same-sex attraction, that is, that there are many factors that interact and contribute to differing degrees from person to person, so that there is no one cause of same-sex attraction that is a key for all persons who report such attractions. See Jones and Yarhouse, *Homosexuality*.
8. Our experience has been that the experiences of same- and opposite-sex attraction are not necessarily linked so that a decrease in same-sex attraction means an increase in opposite-sex attraction. They appear to be best measured by two independent scales.
9. Crystal L. Park & Susan Folkman, "Meaning in the Context of Stress and Coping," *Review of General Psychology*, 1997, Vol. 1, No. 2, pp. 115-144.
10. C. S. Lewis, *A Severe Mercy, Letter to Sheldeon Vanauken* (14 May 1954), chap. 6, p. 147.

Chapter 2: Our Sexuality

1. C. S. Lewis, *The Screwtape Letters* (New York: McMillan, 1967), pp. 137-138.
2. This phrase comes from Michael Mangis and his discussion of unique clusters of "signature sins" with which Christians struggle.
3. R. D. Knudsen, "Images," in Sinclair B. Ferguson, David F. Wright, & J. I. Packer (Eds.), *New Dictionary of Theology* (Downers Grove, IL & Leichester, England: InterVarsity Press, 1988), p. 330.
4. This section draws upon material from Stanton L. Jones and Brenna B. Jones (Date), *How and When to Tell Your Kids about Sex* (Grand Rapids, MI: Baker, 1993).
5. Portions of this section are adapted from Jones and Jones, *How and When*, and Lewis Smedes, *Sex for Christians, second edition* (Grand Rapids, MI: Eerdmans, 1994).
6. Richard Lints, "Imaging and Idolatry: The Sociality of Personhood and the Ironic Reversals of the Canon." Paper presented at the colloquium of the Alliance of Confession Evangelicals, Colorado Springs, Colorado, June, 2002.
7. *Ibid.*, p. 13.

Chapter 3: Myth and Reality about Same-Sex Attraction

1. For recent reviews of this research see Jones and Yarhouse, *Homosexuality*,

Chapter 4; and Susan D. Cochran, "Emerging Issues in Research on Lesbians' and Gay Men's Mental Health: Does Sexual Orientation Really Matter?" *American Psychologist*, 2002, Vol. 56, No. 11, pp. 931-948.

2. Lewis Smedes, *Sex for Christians*.
3. David P. McWhirter and Andrew M. Mattison, *The Male Couple: How Relationships Develop* (Englewood Cliffs, NJ: Prentice-Hall, 1984). See also, A. A. Deenen, L. Gijs, and A. X. van Naerssen, "Intimacy and Sexuality in Gay Male Couples," *Archives of Sexual Behavior*, 1994, Vol. 23, pp. 421-431. Deenen et al. reported on a study of 156 male couples and 62% had had sexual partners outside of the relationship in the past year, with an average of 7.1 sexual partners outside of the relationship.
4. *Ibid.*, p. 285.
5. Robert A. J. Gagnon, *The Bible and Homosexual Practice* (Nashville, TN: Abingdon, 2001).

Chapter 4: Recognizing Patterns

1. Douglas Breunlin, Richard Schwartz, and Betty Mac Kune-Karer, *Metaframeworks, second edition* (New York: Jossey-Bass, 1997).
2. Contact information for these three umbrella organizations is as follows: *Exodus International North America*: P.O. Box 77652, Seattle, WA 98177-0652; phone: (206) 784-7799; Internet: *www.exodusinternational.org*; Homosexuals Anonymous: phone: (610) 376-1146, Internet: http://members.aol.com/hawebpage; Courage: c/o St. John the Baptist Church, 210 West 31st Street, New York, NY 10001, phone: (212) 268-1010; e-mail: *NYCourage@aol.com*; Internet: *HTTP://courageRC.org*.

Chapter 5: Environment Planning

1. Shang-Ding Zhang and W. F. Odenwald, "Misexpression of the White (w) Gene Triggers Male-Male Courtship in Drosophila," *Proceedings of the National Academy of Sciences USA*, 1995, Vol. 92, pp. 5525-5529.
2. For example, in the Stall et al. study, percentages rose from 1.4% (national) to 3.7% (urban) of men who had sex only with males in previous 5 years; additional 2.0% of men had sex with both men and women in the previous 5 years. In the Laumann et al. study, percentages again rose in urban areas as compared to rural: 9.2% (urban) versus 1.3% (rural) or 2.8% (general). These findings were true for self-identifying lesbians as well: 2.6% (urban) versus 1.4% (general) and <1% rural. Although some interpret this as due primarily to migration, these differences are also evidenced among adolescents aged 14-16, so migration alone does not appear to be the cause. For a review of this literature, see Robert A. J. Gagnon, *The Bible and Homosexual Practice* (Lexington, KY: Abingdon, 2001).

3. Michael S. Lundy and George A. Rekers, "Homosexuality in Adolescence: Interventions and Ethical Considerations," in G. A. Rekers (Ed.), *Handbook of Child and Adolescent Sexual Problems* (New York, NY: Lexington, 1995), p. 362.
4. In 1974, the full membership of the American Psychiatric Association voted to follow the 1973 recommendation of its board in officially removing homosexuality from the *Diagnostic and Statistical Manual (DSM)*. Interestingly, Robert Spitzer, who authored the removal of homosexuality from the DSM, recently gave a conference report on 200 persons who claimed to have changed sexual orientation, Spitzer reported that 66% of males and 44% of females reported what he referred to as "good heterosexual functioning" after their change attempt. Good heterosexual functioning was defined as follows: (a) last a year in a loving heterosexual relationship; (b) satisfaction from emotional relationship at least 7+ (1-10 scale); (c) heterosexual sex at least monthly; (d) physical satisfaction from sex at least 7+ (1-10 scale); and never or rarely (<20%) think of same sex during heterosexual sex. These results were nearly identical among the 33 males who were extreme on homosexual indicators prior to their change effort (67% met the criteria for good heterosexual functioning following their change effort; the sample of females was considered too small to provide results). See Robert L. Spitzer, "Two hundred subjects who claim to have changed their sexual orientation from homosexual to heterosexual," in Phillip A. Bialer (Chair), *Clinical Issues and Ethical Concerns Regarding Attempts to Change Sexual Orientation: An Update*. Paper presented at the annual meeting of the American Psychiatric Association, New Orleans, Louisiana, May 9, 2001.
5. Douglas Breunlin, Richard Schwartz, and Betty Mac Kune-Karrer, in their book *Metaframeworks* (San Francisco: Jossey-Bass, 1997) assess and intervene with reference to six overarching frameworks: sequences, organization, culture, gender, development, and internal family systems. While we do not need to embrace this model in order to use the "theory of constraints," the model is noted in case you want to read more about it.
6. Betty Carter and Monica McGoldrick, "Overview: The Expanded Family Life Cycle," in B. Carter & M. McGoldrick (Eds.), *The Expanded Family Life Cycle: Individual, Family, and Social Perspectives* (Needham Heights, MA: Allyn and Bacon, 1999), pp. 1-26.
7. *Ibid.*, p. 362.

Chapter 6: An Exchange: Old Scripts for New

1. Gilbert Herdt, "Developmental Discontinuities and Sexual Orientation Across Cultures," in David P. McWhirter, S. A. Sanders, & J. M. Reinisch (Eds.), *Homosexuality/Heterosexuality: Concepts of Sexual Orientation* (New York: Oxford University Press, 1996), p. 224.

2. Most of the research that addresses the parent-child relationship was published in the 1960s–1980s by people who were committed to a psychoanalytic perspective to begin with. See, for example, Irving Bieber, H. J. Dain, P. R. Dince, M. G Drellich, H. G Grand, R. H. Gundlach, M. W. Kremer, A. H. Rifkin, C. B. Wilber, & T. B. Bieber, *Homosexuality: A Psychoanalytic Study* (New York: Basic Books, 1962); Richard B. Evans, "Childhood Parental Relationships of Homosexual Men," *Journal of Consulting and Clinical Psychology*, 1969, Vol. 33, pp. 129-135. Other studies have not shown the same parent-child dynamic to be correlated with homosexual identification (or have shown another parent-child dynamic), and still other studies have been cited as failing to support the theory, at least they do not provide clear support for it. For example, Alan P. Bell, Martin S. Weinberg, and Sue Kiefer-Hammersmith, *Sexual Preference* (New York: Simon & Schuster, 1980). It may also be the case that the classic "emotionally distant father" and "over-involved mother" may be the result of gender non-conformity in a child.
3. J. W. Robinson, "Understanding the Meaning of Change for Married Latter-Day Saint Men with Histories of Homosexual Activity," unpublished doctoral dissertation. Brigham Young University, 1998.
4. C. M. Ponticelli, "Crafting Stories of Identity Reconstruction," *Social Psychology Quarterly*, 1999, Vol. 62, pp. 157-172.
5. Mike Lew, *Victims No Longer* (New York: Harper Collins, 1990), p. 7.
6. *Ibid.*, p. 7.
7. *Ibid.*, p. 7.
8 Eliana Gil, *Treating Abused Adolescents* (New York: Guilford, 1996), p. 168f.
9. Beverly Engel, *The Right to Innocence: Healing the Trauma of Childhood Sexual Abuse* (New York: Ivy Books, 1989), p. 232.

Chapter 7: Living a Practical Theology of Sanctification

1. Stanton L. Jones, "Identity in Christ and Sexuality," in Timothy Bradshaw (Ed.), *Grace and Truth in the Secular Age* (Grand Rapids, MI: Eerdmans, 1998) p. 100.
2. C. S. Lewis, *The Weight of Glory* (New York: McMillan, 1965), p. 26.
3. *Ibid.*, p. 27.
4. *Ibid.*, p. 28.
5. Dallas Willard, *The Divine Conspiracy* (San Francisco: HarperCollins, 1998), p. 366.
6. *Ibid.*, p. 366.
7. *Ibid.*, p. 366.
8. *Ibid.*, p. 348.
9. G. J. Pigott, "Covetousness," in David J. Atkinson, David F. Field, Arthur Holmes, and Oliver O'Donovan, *New Dictionary of Pastoral Care* (Downers Grove, IL: InterVarsity Press, 1995), p. 267.

10. *Ibid*, p. 267
11. Lewis Smedes, *Sex for Christians, second edition* (Grand Rapids, MI: Eerdmans, 1994).
12. J. H. Olthuis, "Chastity," David J. Atkinson, David F. Field, Arthur Holmes, and Oliver O'Donovan, *New Dictionary of Pastoral Care* (Downers Grove, IL: InterVarsity Press, 1995), p. 223.
13. D. W. Augsburger, "Forgiveness," David J. Atkinson, David F. Field, Arthur Holmes, and Oliver O'Donovan, *New Dictionary of Pastoral Care* (Downers Grove, IL: InterVarsity Press, 1995), p. 389.
14. Pigott, "Covetousness," p.267.
15. Adapted from Smedes, *Sex for Christians*.
16. Olthuis, "Chastity," p. 223.

Chapter 8: A Word to Families

1. Adapted from Ivan Hill (Ed.), *The Bisexual Spouse* (New York: Harper & Row, Publishers, 1987).
2. This section of the chapter is adapted from Mark A. Yarhouse, Lisa M. Pawlowski, and Erica S. N. Tan, "Adversity and Resilience in Marriage: Intact Marriages in which One Partner Experiences Same-Sex Attraction," paper presented at the Christian Association for Psychological Studies East Regional Conference, Bethesda, MD, November 1, 2002.

Chapter 9: A Word to the Church

1. John Stott, *Same-Sex Partnerships? A Christian Perspective* (Grand Rapids, MI: Baker Books, 1998), p. 79.

Index

About the Authors

Mark A. Yarhouse is a licensed clinical psychologist in Virginia and Associate Professor of Psychology at Regent University in Virginia Beach. He received his B.A. degree in Philosophy and Art from Calvin College in 1990, M.A. degree in Clinical Psychology (1993), M.A. degree in Theological Studies (1997), and Psy.D. in Clinical Psychology (1998) from Wheaton College.

Dr. Yarhouse is a member of the American Psychological Association (APA) and a Clinical Member of the American Association for Marriage and Family Therapy (AAMFT). He serves on the editorial boards of the *Journal of Family Violence*, *The Family Journal*, *Journal of Psychology and Theology*, and *Marriage and Family: A Christian Journal*. He is also a consulting editor to *Christian Counseling Today* and serves on the Board of Reference and Advisors for Christian Mental Health Resources (web site).

Dr. Yarhouse chaired a symposium at the annual meeting of the APA where he brought together gay theorists/researchers and conservative religious theorists/researchers to discuss the experiences of homosexual clients who request services to change their sexual orientation. His article from this forum, titled "An inclusive response to LGB and conservative religious persons: The case of same-sex attraction and behavior," was published in *Professional Psychology: Research and Practice*. He presented the paper, "Ethical issues in attempts to ban reorientation therapies" at the annual meeting of the American Psychiatric Association in New Orleans in May 2001. This presentation was published in *Psychotherapy*. Dr. Yarhouse is co-author (with Stanton L. Jones) of *Homosexuality: The Use of Scientific Research in the Church's Moral Debate*, published by InterVarsity Press, and author of the clinical workbook, *Expanding Alternatives to*

Same-Sex Attraction: Clinical Modules for Informed Consent, Assessment, and Intervention. He served as Co-Guest Editor of a two-part theme issue on human sexuality for *Journal of Psychology and Theology.*

Lori A. Burkett is a doctoral candidate in Clinical Psychology at Regent University in Virginia Beach, Virginia. She received the B. A. degree in Psychology and in Sociology with a minor in Criminal Justice from Evangel University in 1992, the M.A. degree in Criminology (1994) from Indiana University of Pennsylvania and the M.A. degree in Clinical Psychology (2001) from Regent University.

Lori is a student member of the American Psychological Association, the Society for the Exploration of Psychotherapy Integration, the American Association for Christian Counselors and the Christian Association for Psychological Studies. Committed to ethical and effective treatment, Lori invests time in various research endeavors and is published in peer-review journals. She has presented at numerous regional and national conferences on topics related to sexuality, trauma, integration of psychology and theology, and supervision and consultation.